Praise for *Serving Mo*

"Too often the topic of stewardship is avoided in th̲e̲_
rarely is stewardship addressed as a topic of justice. Dr. Sheryl Johnson
makes the case that an intertwined theology of stewardship and justice
is essential for the future of the church. And she's right. Religious
leaders should take note. The future of our faith communities depends
on it."

—**David P. King,** Karen Lake Buttrey Director,
Lake Institute on Faith & Giving, Indiana University
Lilly Family School of Philanthropy

"This book stands in the tragic gap between our gospel values and our
financial practices as churches. Speaking both pastorally and prophetically, Johnson offers practical and theologically grounded wisdom
for how congregations can make financial decisions that reflect their
deepest values and commitments. A must-read for pastors, finance
committees, and church boards."

—**The Very Reverend Jordan Cantwell,**
former moderator, United Church of Canada

"Sheryl Johnson's book is a shining gift to the North American
church of our day. It is a prophetic, pragmatic guiding light for faith
communities who hunger to align their practices—including financial
practices—with their faith in a God who is bringing life in its fullness
to all. With crystal clarity and compassionate wisdom, Johnson invites
congregations and denominations to root practices regarding money—
raising, spending, saving, redistributing it—in faith. She guides the
reader through a journey into church finance through a lens of spiritual
integrity and liberation. The journey is theologically rooted and spiritually inspired, and it profiles congregations that are working to align
finances with their faith commitments. This delightfully conversational
book will enable the church to move more fully into its vocation,
practice the gospel, and live incarnationally. Read this book! It is
invaluable."

—**Cynthia Moe-Lobeda,** author of *Resisting Structural Evil:
Love as Ecological-Economic Vocation*

"When money is seen as a theological matter, faith communities can address much of the shallowness and frustration that plague religious life today. In this book, Sheryl Johnson provides valuable suggestions for deepening faith and life with an eye toward what truly matters, initiating courageous conversations that are still in short supply."

—**Joerg Rieger,** distinguished professor of theology, Vanderbilt University

"Sheryl Johnson bravely addresses the current Lazarus-like chasm between justice commitments and church finances. With an encouraging tone of humility and hope, Johnson offers both analysis and principles, but pushes beyond to make practical suggestions as to how churches can begin to incarnate justice-based Christian stewardship in a time such as this."

—**Jennifer Henry,** senior program development and strategy lead, United Church of Canada

"Johnson offers an accessible roadmap and focalizing handbook for how (and why) mainstream churches can prioritize the gospel over the dominant economic story, and find new life amid hard times through personal and institutional practices of economic solidarity and justice."

—**Ched Myers,** author of *The Biblical Vision of Sabbath Economics*, and co-director of Bartimaeus Cooperative Ministries

"Examples abound in this book. The theology is sound and simple. Sheryl Johnson's book is a deep but easy read. It is concise while comprehensive. Here is multidimensional, multicultural generosity that is applicable to churches small and large. It is moving and motivating."

—**William Green,** author of *52 Ways to Ignite Your Congregation: Generous Giving,* and former director of stewardship and church finances, United Church of Christ

"Drawing from her church experience, Johnson challenges today's congregations to assess how they raise, spend, invest, give away, and make decisions regarding money. She prods them to build practices grounded in Christian theology, ethics, and faith, rather than in secular fundraising, neoliberal capitalism, and contemporary US cultural beliefs and practices, to align their faith with their financial behavior.

She illuminates both the past and present while giving examples to help imagine a different future. She writes not from on high but with humility and in a relational style. Viewing the decline witnessed in many churches as an opportunity for creative transformation, she invites 'us to recognize and embrace the new life God is offering us.' *Serving Money, Serving God* is a thought-provoking and ground-breaking contribution."

>—**Rev. Dr. David Cleaver-Bartholomew, PhD,** director of stewardship and donor relations, Southern New England Conference, United Church of Christ

"Despite vigorous and prophetic challenges to neoliberalism made by religious leaders, by ecumenical and interfaith organizations, and within many congregations, most stewardship campaigns continue to reflect market-oriented approaches to wealth creation and the distribution of financial gifts. Sheryl Johnson's book provides a desperately needed, creative, and justice-oriented approach that will challenge you to think about stewardship as far more than a campaign or program—it is a way of life and reflects the distinctive witness and identity of Christian ministry and mission. *Serving Money, Serving God* is an accessible and essential read for religious leaders hoping to put their ethical commitments into action."

>—**Elizabeth Hinson-Hasty,** professor of theology and religious studies, Bellarmine University, and author of *The Problem of Wealth: A Christian Response to a Culture of Affluence*

SERVING MONEY
SERVING GOD

Aligning Radical Justice,
Christian Practice,
and Church Life

SERVING
MONEY

SERVING
GOD

Sheryl
Johnson

FORTRESS PRESS

MINNEAPOLIS

SERVING MONEY, SERVING GOD
Aligning Radical Justice, Christian Practice, and Church Life

Cover design: Kristin Miller
Cover image: "Abstract color acrylic and watercolor painting" © rudchenko,
Getty Images 1279006837

Print ISBN: 978-1-5064-8296-5
eBook ISBN: 978-1-5064-8297-2

Territorial Acknowledgment

I have researched, reflected, learned, and written this book on the territory of xučyun (Huichin), the ancestral and unceded land of the Chochenyo-speaking Ohlone people, the successors of the historic and sovereign Verona Band of Alameda County.[1]

Contents

Preface

I never imagined I'd write a book like this. Christian stewardship has always been off-putting to me, at best boring and at worst an impediment to what drew me to church in the first place. I thought of stewardship as primarily about the institution rather than the mission of the church. As a youth, when I became active in my local United Church of Canada (UCC) congregation, it was the intersection of faith and justice that spoke to me. God's call of liberation for all people and all of creation rang in my ears, and the church's long and global witness to this work was a lineage I was proud to join. I was proud of my denomination's history of being on the frontlines of so many movements for social justice. In the church, I found a community where all the issues I cared about came together and the biblical story offered deep insight into humanity's long struggles for justice and liberation. I adored the intergenerational, intercultural, international community of church and the spiritual practices which connected us and sustained us in this work. But as I was invited into formal church leadership, the questions and issues I often saw leaders engaging with felt so disconnected from this vibrant work for justice. So much time was spent focusing on issues arising from declining membership. It seemed like there was an unspoken agreement that we needed to ensure institutional survival by whatever means necessary and an assumption that survival would require cutting the very programs and work that had drawn me into the church. Other leaders seemed to view justice work as expensive, without much (financial or membership) "return on investment." Justice work was worth doing, but was ultimately optional when money was tight.

Again and again, I have returned to questions about the relationship between the internal practices and structures of churches and their broader values, ethics, and commitments to justice. This has particularly been the case as I have grappled with my various forms of privilege, which include my race (I am a white settler and colonizer on Indigenous lands), global location (Canada and the United States), religion (mainline Christian—United Church of Canada/United Church of Christ), class (middle/upper-middle class), ability, and educational attainment. I experience significant advantages in most contexts, privileges that have afforded me access and opportunity, but that also mean there is much I do not know firsthand about marginalization. I believe much of my privilege has been not only unearned but also unjustly granted through systemic factors such as white supremacy, European colonization, neoliberal capitalism, and Christian dominance.

This book has its roots in many personal experiences I have had in church, many of which you'll read about. But I want to begin with the experience that led me to devote years of my life to the disconnect between values and financial practices, an encounter I had as a seminary student preparing for ordained ministry in the United Church of Canada. The story takes place in 2012 when my now-spouse and I served as ministry interns with the National Council of Churches of the Philippines (NCCP). The internship was an incredible experience, and I am deeply grateful for the hospitality of our many hosts and the prophetic theological work for justice I encountered. While many internships involve a lot of skill-building, our experience in the Philippines was more focused on exposure and learning, visiting many organizations and attending numerous conferences, but not much "work." This is because the NCCP has a strong commitment to its own autonomy and agency. Members believe that the expertise and skill needed to do their work exists within the Philippines, and they do not allow visitors to work for them. But interns from the Global North are welcomed to come to learn—and then go back to their home countries to do advocacy on the issues they have learned about.

The NCCP is one of many global partner organizations with which the UCC has an ongoing relationship. Many of these global partner relationships evolved out of former missionary relationships. Over time, the UCC (like other mainline denominations) has worked to reimagine its global church relationships and to increase its understanding of the inequality between the Global North and the Global South. It has moved away from an older "missionary" model focused on conversion and unidirectional mission (the idea that those in the Global North are the only ones who have gifts, such as faith, education, and practical skills to offer) and toward a model of dialectic partnership. In this new type of global relationship, the United Church and its partners name and recognize power imbalances and systemic injustice, seek mutuality in mission, and together critique the Global North and its churches. Partners such as the NCCP are invited to participate in UCC decision-making, and the UCC gives block (rather than program-specific) grants to the NCCP and other partner organizations, allowing them to use funds as they see fit. The model of offering block grants is an attempt to offer consistent funding year to year (allowing longer-range planning) and both an acknowledgment of and a response to the global systemic injustices that have led to wealth disparity between the Global North and the Global South.

When I was in the Philippines, I had the privilege of hearing about the relationship between the UCC and the NCCP from my NCCP hosts. I remember their spacious, cool office building—a respite from the heat and bustle of the Quezon City area of Manila where they are located. I remember the day that our NCCP liaison explained to me why their office space was so large—it used to house over two hundred staff. However, when I was an intern in 2012, only about twenty people were employed. My hosts shared that this was due, in part, to declines in funding support from their ecumenical church partners in the Global North. As NCCP's work had shifted in the 1980s and 1990s toward greater involvement in systemic and political causes of injustice in the Philippines, some of their church partners reduced their funding support. The NCCP staff described the pressure they felt to focus on natural disaster relief. Churches and other donors are willing to provide funds for such efforts, but not for projects that address the root causes of suffering and inequality. "But not the UCC," our hosts said emphatically. They told me the UCC had been one of their most faithful partners, providing ongoing financial support that gave them the autonomy to use the funding as they saw fit. "Plus, they are the reason why we have a photocopier, no one else would fund that for us." They believed the UCC had been receptive to their analysis of power and injustice issues in the world. They saw this as a sign of true mutuality and partnership. While this praise was generous and an honor to hear, it also made me want to cry. Only a few months prior to my internship, I had been part of a meeting of the United Church's General Council Executive at which decisions were made to address budget shortfalls by (among other things) reducing these block grants to global partners. Despite its commitments, the denomination was also beginning to introduce programs that would allow individuals and congregations to direct funds to specific partners and projects in hopes it would increase their total giving.

When back in Canada, I saw that both local and global church partner organizations, including the NCCP and others I was connected to, were increasingly being required to fundraise for their own budgets due to denominational cuts, in some ways competing with one another. I was involved with several organizations that had received block grants from the UCC, and most of these organizations were informed that these grants would be declining in size and might not continue in the future. I saw these organizations dedicate increasing amounts of time to applying for grants, developing donor databases, reaching out to regional church bodies and wealthy congregations for funds, and, in many cases, reducing their staffing and programming. I also saw how much easier this transition was for some organizations than for others. Some organizations had significant access to a logical base of supporters with financial means (for example, a university chaplaincy in a large, wealthy city), while others struggled to adapt to this new arrangement (for example, a community outreach organization serving marginalized populations in a region with less overall wealth). Wealth inequality among churches was also on my mind as I looked for work upon graduation from seminary, seeing churches in wealthier neighborhoods advertising for associate ministers while those in poorer communities often had postings for only one part-time minister. Although sometimes those churches had smaller membership, this was not the only factor that determined their staffing arrangements.

In a denomination committed to principles such as economic and racial justice, I was surprised not to find discussion of these disparities either in seminary or among denominational leaders. This commitment was a major aspect of what excited me and many of my seminary classmates about ministry. In seminary, we talked about church decline, but rarely did we consider which churches were likely to be impacted by decline, nor did we talk about the overall ramifications for our church's commitments to social justice. And when I got into congregational ministry after seminary, taking one of those associate minister positions in a wealthy congregation, my sense of disconnect deepened. The congregation I served was deeply faithful and passionate about social justice, but financial decisions were seen as separate from justice work. And when the stewardship and finance leaders looked for resources, they found support for maintaining this disconnect rather than ideas for bridging it.

This book is my offering to that church, the others I've served, and all my siblings seeking justice and liberation through progressive Christianity. Leaders in congregations and other church-related organizations, and church members more generally, have long rooted our financial practices in values that serve money while striving to serve God through our faith. I hope this book will help us imagine how our financial practices are integral to our faith, and can help us serve God.

Acknowledgments

This book has been in no way a solitary project. I am so grateful to the many communities and individuals who have supported, critiqued, and inspired me on the journey. I am particularly grateful for my wonderful doctoral advisor, Dr. Cynthia Moe-Lobeda, and my many other faculty mentors and student colleagues at Graduate Theological Union who were integral to my dissertation research project. One of the outcomes of that project is this book, designed to initiate a broader conversation on its topic.

I am also appreciative for the many churches and faith communities that have supported me as I have thought about these ideas and developed this project: the Congregational Church of San Mateo, the United Church of Christ, the United Church of Canada, the Student Christian Movement/World Student Christian Federation, the National Council of Churches of the Philippines, Agape Fellowship, and Circle of Hope. I am grateful to all the pastors and ministry leaders who graciously gave their time and allowed me to interview them, and particularly Marguerite McDonald and Sarah Pritchard, who agreed to be quoted.

Thank you to everyone at Fortress Press for your support and for the opportunity and privilege to create this project, and especially to Beth Gaede for making my writing sharper and arguments clearer.

In the writing of this book specifically, I was supported by many excellent conversation partners and draft readers, especially Dannis Matteson and my spouse Kelly Colwell. Kelly: in writing, in ministry, and in life I could ask for no better collaborator and partner.

Finally, I am grateful to have been formed by many progressive Christian communities and a justice-seeking faith tradition. I write from a place of abiding love and deep commitment. For this and so much else, thanks be to God.

Introduction

Two Masters: God and Money

In progressive churches, we love to celebrate diversity. Race, gender, sexual orientation, religion, age, disability, and so forth: we lift up all of these as aspects of the beauty of God's diverse creation, intended by God as part of the divine design. Sometimes we include class and economic differences in that list of diverse characteristics. Of course, God cares for us all, but does God really create us as rich and poor? Or are wealth and poverty the outcomes of oppressive systems that a liberating God commands us to work against—systems such as racism, colonialism, patriarchy, and neoliberal capitalism? Does God really intend for some to have too little and some to have far more than too much? How does excessive wealth create poverty? When we look around our churches and communities, our nations, and the world, we can't help but realize how much of an economic divide exists. This situation is even more unsettling when we realize how those economic divisions fall along lines of other social factors such as race—a reality we name as sin.[1]

Not everyone will agree with me that wide wealth disparity is contrary to God's will. If that's you, this isn't your book. If you believe in the prosperity gospel and that God rewards good people with money, this book won't make a lot of sense to you. I am writing for those of us who believe that inequality is a spiritual problem. Maybe you aren't quite sure how to address it, but the idea that our relationship with God inevitably leads us to work for social justice resonates with you. If that makes sense to you, then you and I are co-conspirators in this work, and I am grateful for that. And I am grateful that we get to try to figure out what to do about it together. We are not alone!

When we look to the church, we easily see that congregations are not all the same. Some are wealthier than others, and some are more economically diverse than others. But the fact remains that mainline churches tend to be privileged.[2] This fact itself deserves critical analysis. Those of us who work and worship in these settings have much to learn from the economic solidarity and prophetic work being done in more marginalized church communities. I am deeply grateful for the ways these communities have shaped my theological and ecclesial imagination of what is possible and what our faith calls us all toward.

This book is written primarily for churches with privilege, especially in its racial and economic forms. It is also an invitation for those of us in predominantly privileged settings to move toward solidarity by considering our own practices and how we might bring them in line with our ideals, and even more importantly, our faith.

A Church That Embodies What It Believes?

At a 2008 denominational event for young adults I attended, the former moderator of the United Church of Canada, David Giuliano, shared that in his travels across Canada during his leadership term he often met with young people not currently active in church. Many would say to him something like, "I love everything the United Church has done around radical inclusion and on the front lines of social justice struggles. I love its statements about important social issues. I'd love to be a part of a church that embodies this. Can you recommend a congregation to me?" As he told us this story, Giuliano admitted that he often wasn't sure how to respond or which church to recommend. He knew so many congregations were primarily concerned with their own survival, preoccupied with worries about their aging buildings and grief regarding past glories which were now a distant memory. Even churches that did engage in work for justice often did so in a segmented way. Justice work was often seen merely as a side program of the church with an outward focus, rather than core to their mission and identity, with these values deeply informing all aspects of the congregation's life. Still, Giuliano shared this story with the young adults gathered as a hopeful one: the theology of progressive churches resonates with many people, and the history of social and political engagement is inspiring even to those who are not currently involved. Potential and possibility exist, but translating that progressive theology into practical congregational life has thus far eluded many of us.

At the same time, the connection between beliefs and practices, faith and action, is often celebrated as a hallmark of progressive Christianity. This engagement takes many forms: sermons that promote community service, civic engagement, and social justice as important to Christian discipleship; congregational activities, such as supporting food banks and even attending protests and marches for social and ecological justice; and, particularly at a denominational level, adopting prophetic statements that articulate theological support for seeking justice through public policy and action. While these commitments and activities are important to church identity, they are often approached as programs that engage broader society but are not expected to shape internal church life and practice as well. These commitments generally focus "outward" toward "others," locating the church in the role of a benevolent figure that should assist as it is able—but not primarily as an actor that is implicated in systems of oppression or facing significant issues of injustice internally. The church itself is largely presented and understood as a neutral space, and any engagement for justice is viewed as a net positive.

The reality is so much more complex. But the work to integrate justice into all aspects of church life matters. And scholars confirm that Giuliano's experience with young people seeking churches committed to justice is widespread. A 2016 Pew research study found that one in five people who left their childhood religion did so due to a dislike of organized religion, for reasons including pervasive hierarchy and religious communities operating too much like businesses.[3] This is similar to the findings of a 2009 Pew research study that found that about 50 percent of those who had become unaffiliated with religion had done so because they found religious people "hypocritical, judgmental, or insincere."[4] We can see in this research that an alignment between belief and action has serious practical implications, particularly considering the current rate of church decline and the rise of religious "nones." But the work of integrating justice into church finances isn't a growth strategy. It stands on its own merits and is the right thing to do, even if it turns some people away.

The Divide Between Faith and Practice

In my experience, many church members don't immediately see a divide between their congregation's beliefs and practices. They quickly point to beloved programs that serve their local community, congregational attendance at protests, building space rented to community groups, and sermons and prayers that name injustices in the world. All of this work is important, and I do not mean to minimize its value. But I will consider many other aspects of church life. I will warn you: the list may seem daunting. Take heart, though. I am not going to list "sins" and then give up or leave you to face it on your own. The first step toward practicing our faith and engaging ethics is to name the gaps between what we believe and what we do. If you find yourself getting defensive in this section, take note of that response. It may help you identify what topics, such as race-based reparations or the notion that what you have is rightfully yours, you need to pay special attention to. Some of us are already attending to some of these concerns in our churches, although hardly any of us are attending to all of them.

In most contexts, we should be asking questions about the traditional Indigenous territory where the church is situated and examining how the church is culpable in the colonization, occupation, and subjugation of Indigenous peoples, spiritualities, and lands. We should be exploring how predominantly white churches have contributed to the racial and economic segregation and inequality of neighborhoods and cities.[5] We should be considering the carbon footprint of church facilities and church life more generally.

We should be asking questions of the economic (and other aspects of) inequality among members within churches, where we preach about bearing one another's burdens and being one united body, knowing some church members struggle to pay for life's essentials while others have more than enough to meet their needs and wants. When we compare churches, we should be asking why some churches, predominantly white, have significant budgets, with many paid staff, large endowments, and a great capacity to generate rental income, while other churches, predominantly nonwhite, have no paid staff and own no property. The list of potential divides between beliefs and practices goes on and on.

But in my experience, these questions are rarely asked. Instead, we take for granted that individual congregations, like individual people, are largely responsible for their own finances (and not for those of others). If they have wealth, we believe they have generated it themselves through merit (and perhaps even faithfulness) and that it is therefore completely at their disposal. We assume that churches having more members and more money can be taken as a sign of successful and important ministry, while having fewer members or less money is a sign of failure of mission, or a failure to adapt to the times—rather than, perhaps, a sign of systemic inequality. More—more property, larger budgets, larger membership—is always assumed to be better than less. We, as individuals and congregations, take for granted that if we own property, it is rightfully ours and we think no further questions need to be asked about matters such as how it was acquired, who it was acquired from, and what this ownership has meant and means. We may want to install solar panels or build a wheelchair ramp (at least into the sanctuary, perhaps to access the entire building, including the pulpit), but we feel no great sense of urgency. It seems okay to exist as we are, at least for now. Truisms such as "we can't do it all" lead to complacency. We often simply accept that church life as we know it costs money, and therefore we should use the "best" methods out there to raise as much as we can so we can "get on" to "doing church"—worship, pastoral care, and so forth—and, ideally, expand and increase what we do.

Typical Christian Stewardship

Budgeting, financial management, and fundraising— or "stewardship," as these are often called—are church practices that require ethical scrutiny. And they are part of "doing church," not simply a precursor to it. Many books written about these topics assume that more is always better, that minimizing expenses that don't yield quantifiable returns and maximizing income are the two best ways to get to that goal, and that conventional best practices are ethically neutral. The aspects of ministry that don't yield financial returns are often those most associated with justice work: contributing to community organizations and partners, meeting the practical needs of marginalized community members, and carrying out the work of the wider church (which is varied, but may include national advocacy work and grants for marginalized or struggling congregations, and so forth). Stewardship consultants advise church leaders to be prudent about our expenditures and seek out the lowest costs wherever possible: purchasing the cheapest goods (regardless of social and environmental impacts); outsourcing work (for example, using a custodial service, where employees are often very underpaid people of color); hiring ministers, administrative staff, musicians, and so on for the bare minimum of hours (often fewer than they will actually work) and lowest wages when we do employ people; and relying on volunteers (often women) wherever possible.

To maximize income, we are told to keep our financial messages positive and upbeat ("no one wants to give to a dying institution!"), spend special time with top donors and the wealthy to cultivate gifts that align with their interests, and simply emphasize proportional giving to deal with economic differences/inequality, not attending to the fact that some members may not have enough to meet even their most basic needs. We accept that what we raise within our congregation is ours to do with as we wish, and we don't generally think we owe anything to anyone else. If we do happen to give to an individual or organization in the community (or even our denomination or other church organization), we expect an expression of gratitude no matter how small the measure of our support. Often churches create requirements for the funding they may offer, stating that the need must align with "our" priorities and requiring extensive applications/reports from the recipient. These stipulations may be due to congregations' desires to further their missions, handle their resources responsibly, and fairly discern how to respond to requests, but when priorities are largely determined by privileged folks and congregations, this practice needs to be carefully evaluated. Do requirements for application materials and reporting documents place undue burdens on the people and organizations we say we want to help? Many potential recipients have limited time to devote to this work, and we need to remember that they may need to complete multiple iterations of these documents as they piece together funding from a variety of sources, each with their own requirements.

The processes by which churches obtain and manage funds have been generally understood even by very social justice–oriented Christians as largely outside the realm of social justice commitments—a neutral precondition to church work rather than an essential part of it that should be subject to the same ethical scrutiny these churches apply to issues in society and the world more broadly. Any positive "ends" resulting from a congregation's ministry are generally assumed to justify the "means," meaning a church's economic practices are not examined carefully. When ethical considerations do come into play, they often focus on financial mismanagement, embezzlement, or other criminalized acts—or, at best, considerations of ethical investment/unethical divestment (regarding companies engaged in producing weapons or fossil fuels, for example). These concerns are important, but, since much attention has already been paid to preventing mismanagement and changing investing practices, they will not be the primary focus of this book. Such actions are good and faithful, but they're not enough. Our commitments to social and ecological justice should shape every aspect of church life and practice, not just our investing and our money management.

Addressing every aspect of church life and practice is too much to do in one book, of course. This book is about money in church, and I hope it will challenge you to think about the ways we raise, make decisions about, spend, save, and redistribute it. Instead of adopting practices from secular fundraising theories, I want to challenge us to build practices that are rooted in our faith convictions. This goal might be raising some defenses already, because often those in charge of church finances are those with professional business or finance experience, which might mean seeing free-market capitalist approaches as value-neutral, the best or even only way to approach money. People with those backgrounds might also see this approach as appropriate to church financial life, even in progressive churches that actively critique the harmful impact of neoliberal capitalism, the economic system that is so mainstream, many of us hardly notice it.

A Tale of Two Churches

As I was growing up, I think I assumed all churches were more or less alike. Of course, I knew some churches were bigger and fancier, while others were smaller and simpler. I assumed that megachurches had more money because they had more members and figured that maybe because they really wanted to get people in the door, they spent on fancy things they thought would attract people. But then, throughout my university and seminary education, I worked part-time in several congregations, mostly with children and youth. And I began to learn that the economic differences between churches were about so much more than their membership size—or may have little to do with size at all.

One church where I worked was in a more economically precarious neighborhood, and the church itself had relatively limited means. They rented space to a number of community organizations throughout the week, and on Sundays, a series of primarily ethnic-specific immigrant church communities (which were viewed primarily as necessary sources of income) worshipped in their sanctuary following a strict schedule. Still, the church budget was always tight. In getting to know a few members from some of these renting church communities, as I quickly tidied up craft supplies on Sundays (so they could use the space after me), I realized how my church, as the property owner, had much greater power and privilege (even with our financial constraints). We had the first pick of worship times, use of most of the space, even though we had fewer members than many of the renting churches, and I was paid, while the renting churches had only volunteer children and youth leaders (and, in some cases, unpaid pastors as well).

A few years later, I worked at a different church in a wealthier neighborhood. There were still some rental groups, but these paid quite well (due to the nicer neighborhood and the beautiful, recently renovated facilities), and the schedule of rentals never felt chaotic or packed. As a youth minister, I had an ample weekly budget to buy food for the youth to eat during our programs. But most of the youth looked somewhat disdainfully upon what I bought, letting me know they were going to a restaurant for brunch after or had just been to the coffee shop on their way in. I thought about how at my previous church, having a budget to buy food might have really made a difference to the kids who attended. I thought about the churches that rented space from my old church and remembered the elaborate post-worship meals I had been invited to and wondered if those had been a financial stretch for them to host.

At my new church, I was told to never let cost be a barrier for any kids, no matter the activity—summer camp, outings, trips. The congregation generously supported people within their own church community, yet rarely did any family request this assistance or seem to need it. I remembered the relentless fundraisers we held at the previous church, one baked good at a time, to send just one child to camp. I reflected on what I heard preached in both churches, that we are one in Jesus, one family in Christ. Although both churches talked about being part of one global church family, it seemed the financial obligations stopped at the door—or even closer than "the door," with the renting churches that used the same physical space largely viewed as just a means to get closer to balancing the budget rather than fellow Christians with a shared mission and faith. As I got to know families better in both churches, I realized that while members often shared in times of prayer certain health concerns (though rarely naming other issues related to health, such as addiction and mental illness), many stressors, especially about money, were not shared aloud. We preached that we wanted to bear one another's burdens, but it was simply assumed that a lack of money was a private burden to bear alone. Both churches—and individuals within them—contributed to various community organizations and gave to the denomination, but these were not really seen as core necessities.

It was understood by members and leaders as a noble thing to do, but the primary responsibility was to balance the internal, individual church budget.

These two churches were not that far from each other, both located in the same city. In fact, I later learned some people who lived in my first church's neighborhood attended the wealthier second church. At the second church, they were proud of this fact and celebrated that people often traveled across the city to attend (subtly implying that they were "outcompeting" other churches). I wondered why families chose to travel to attend a different church of the same denomination. Of course, people have many reasons for doing this, but sometimes wealthier churches just seem to get wealthier—having the programs, staff, facilities, and so forth to easily attract new members—while the struggling churches just struggle more, even facing the possibility of closure. But when church closures were discussed in settings like my seminary classes, issues like class and race never seemed to come up. We talked about church closures as though they were happening randomly all over, and church decline as though it was evenly spread. We talked a lot about how closures might not be so bad—God might be doing a new thing—and about how buildings were an expensive burden anyway. While themes of privilege and oppression were central in discussions of most of our courses, from Bible to theology to pastoral care, they were notably absent when church administration and logistics came up. How might those conversations have been different if issues were viewed through a lens informed by social justice?

Overview

This book will examine church finance from a critical and countercultural standpoint—through the lenses of justice and liberation. I hope it will equip progressive church leaders and members to live out their justice commitments in the practices of their churches. I will identify and offer some suggestions to bridge the gulf between progressive justice commitments and everyday church practices. I will call on the church to live fully into its vocation, to exercise integrity that reflects the gospel, and to live incarnationally, putting our faith into practice.

In chapter 1 I'll remind readers of who we say we are and what we are striving to be—our ethical commitments, frameworks, and "sources" for communal discernment, such as scripture, history, theology, and contemporary frameworks, including intersectionality and decoloniality. In chapter 2 I look at some of the values and assumptions common in Christian stewardship and church finance. As we together unpack some of the ways these common practices (even in progressive churches) don't align with our commitments to justice, in chapter 3 we'll explore specific aspects of church life (property, buildings, and so forth) that deserve to be reconsidered. Moving back to a broader perspective, in chapter 4 I write about what Christian finance and stewardship could be when informed by our commitments. Then, in chapter 5, I profile communities and organizations that are working to align their internal finances with their broader commitments to justice, suggesting how this can really work. In chapter 6 I offer some theological concepts I find helpful, inviting you—personally and as part of various communities—to consider how you might be called in this work.

God and Money

In progressive churches, we are often (rightly) critical of dualisms and binaries. The bifurcation between body and mind/spirit, sacred and profane, and so forth has often been used to support oppressive hierarchies and to view God as completely separated from the world (another such dualism). Challenging distinctions between ministry and administration, mission and maintenance, faith and institution are at the heart of this book. However, there is also a time and place for bold affirmation and rejection—prophetic yeses and nos that may in fact involve some binary oppositions. The biblical texts about serving God and money contains one of those. In Matthew 6:24 we hear: "No one can serve two masters; for a slave will either hate the one and love the other, or be devoted to the one and despise the other. You cannot serve God and wealth."

I am not saying money can never be used for God's work, but I do believe our primary orientation must be one of skepticism toward money and the values and practices that often surround it. Every form of inequality and injustice in our world, from racism to climate change to ableism and beyond, is manifest in economic inequality and arises, at least in part, from our economic structures and systems. For those of us steeped in privilege (be that racial, economic, or otherwise) we must reckon with how our privilege and power have been gained, at least in large part, through unjust systems. Our privilege may also mean that we do not notice the harm that our lifestyles and economic structures perpetuate as readily as those with less power do. We must reorient our lives and our practices around God and God's values, rather than those of money. This will require us to swim upstream against a strong current, and people may tell us that we are foolish, or something worse, for trying to do so. We will likely fall short of our visions. But I believe that God is with us in this work and delights in our efforts. Many saints (official and unofficial) accompany us along the way. Those oppressed by the dominant systems have given us their testimonies and witness to show why this work matters. And our faith compels us.

1.

God's Call to Justice

Examining Our Values and Commitments

Connecting our values and commitments to our church practices requires us to know—deeply—what our values and commitments are. But both knowing and connecting are more complicated than they may seem on the surface. I'm sure I'm not the only one to attend church meetings that open with a prayer, a devotion, a reading of a mission statement, or even a short time of worship—all ways of naming our beliefs and our vision of what could and should be—but then quickly move on to business as usual in a way that seems completely disconnected from the meeting's start. I think many of us experience this pattern in our personal lives as well. We learn about an issue of injustice, pledge sincerely to do our part to address it, but then, the next thing we know, there we are, falling back into our usual habits and practices. Knowing our commitments deeply enough to integrate them into our regular practices will require more than intellectual knowing and well-intentioned preaching and prayers. How can we immerse ourselves in spaces, communities, and practices that will help us be accountable to our values, rather than allow us to default into our society's mainstream financial patterns?

Meetings aren't the only arena where we can connect our values and commitments to our actions, but because so many of our financial decisions are made in meetings, let's start there with an exercise for the imagination. Imagine a gathering of decision-makers who are diverse in age, gender, race, economic status, and relationship to the church. Imagine prophetic artwork on the wall or maybe a gathering outdoors. Imagine a simple agenda with lots of time. Imagine beginning with an Indigenous land acknowledgment, including current events from the media and our own pastoral concerns in our devotional time, and returning to prayer throughout the meeting, reminding ourselves continually of our purpose. Imagine the feeling of making decisions about money in that space with those people.

Next, imagine meeting in a corporate-feeling space, primarily with people with business experience and wealth, working through a packed agenda in a rushed way. Imagine beginning with a vote to accept the minutes from the last meeting, focusing exclusively on budgetary concerns to the exclusion of other church activities and spiritual practices.

Which of these imaginary meetings might truly empower decision-makers to connect practices with values?

Of course, changing our meeting styles can get us only part of the way there. To bring our values into our practices, we need to focus on the ones that we want to guide our thinking about our church practices. But we can remind ourselves of those values through tangible symbols. In the field of ethics, we talk about "sources" for our ethical deliberation, which remind us of who we are and what we value most. Those sources carry authority and help us know how we should behave. We always engage multiple sources, knowing that bringing different perspectives into conversation often yields a more nuanced and complex result. Different traditions and denominations may give more weight to some sources than others, but Christians typically draw on Scripture, theology, history, and church statements as some of our core "sources."

Scripture

Theologians and ethicists who write about Christian economic ethics look to a wide variety of texts and themes in scripture, and many biblical scholars have also underscored the economic and social implications that arise from the Bible. When we are rooted in a commitment to justice, we see connections in scripture everywhere, even in texts not commonly used in conversations about money or justice. Every time we read the Bible or prepare or listen to a sermon, we can ask ourselves, What might this mean for the financial practices of our church? What radical vision might this passage invite us into?

For me, a central story that underpins my understanding of church economic practices is the description of the early Christian community in Acts 2, where we see that one of the first practical responses to the story and life of Jesus is the communal commitment to holding all things—all possessions—in common. What might that mean if we, as church members, tried to think of our possessions and resources as not for us alone but belonging to the entire community—church or otherwise? A basic example of this mindset is church potluck meals, where each person who is able brings a dish to share but all are invited to the table, whether they have contributed or not. Sometimes leftovers are distributed to those most in need, either in the church community or more broadly. But churches can and do live into this text in other ways—each contributing to the offering plate as we are able and then allocating and distributing the funds through mutual discernment. Some churches host lending libraries of books, tools, toys, or other items. While these examples don't involve holding *all* of our possessions in common, they do involve "commoning" some part of our resources, at least in our local church community.

Some people hear about this practice in Acts and feel skeptical, and for good reason. To not have any private possessions, to not have a way out of the community if we need one, can be a tremendous act of vulnerability. In cults and other forms of abusive relationships, people (particularly of lower status) are often not allowed to have their own possessions as a tool of control. Holding things in common is a risky proposition, and we need to be careful about people's vulnerability and the potential for manipulation. But I wonder if we respond to that concern by defaulting too quickly to primarily viewing our possessions as our own. Perhaps we could live with a creative tension between respecting agency and striving to redistribute resources justly to all, trying to correct for the imbalances created by structural inequalities. What might it mean for us to "common" more of our resources, to view our primary responsibility as not simply for ourselves and our immediate families? Might we extend our care to the young person we vowed to support in baptism, who is now going into deep debt to pay for education, or the recently unemployed person experiencing a medical crisis, whom we have prayed for and even delivered a meal to?

We can also turn to the Hebrew Bible and see practices such as sabbath and jubilee, gleaning laws (requirements to leave some fruit in one's orchards unpicked for people in need to take freely), restrictions on usury (unjust lending), and requirements to care for society's marginalized—in biblical times, groups such as orphans, widows, and foreigners, who were particularly vulnerable. Theologian Ched Myers's work on sabbath economics is a beautiful exploration into the contemporary economic implications of these texts. Myers argues that churches often "spiritualize" the Bible's economic messages, overlooking (or even avoiding) the practical implications,[1] such as God's call for us to deconstruct unjust systems and to redistribute and reallocate resources from the privileged to the poor and marginalized.[2] What might such a practice look like for our churches, denominations, and communities? For example, might congregations that have accumulated so much more than others (often along lines like race and class) feel a call to redistribute some of that accumulation?

Christian Theology

Some notions from Christian theology are also useful as sources for making decisions about justice in church finance. But we need not limit ourselves to theological tenets that specifically address money and possessions. When we consider what financial structures and practices are fitting for churches, what we believe about God matters. As I said in the introduction, if we believe God rewards "good" people with material resources, a claim that is a part of the phenomenon known as the "prosperity gospel," one implication is that inequality isn't a human-created problem but is simply part of God's design. While that belief is generally critiqued in progressive churches, elements of it still show up at times. Have you ever heard in an offering prayer, "God, you gave us everything we have; now receive these offerings as a sign of our gratitude"? Even the notion that God has given each of us our material possessions individually can imply that God wants some of us to have more than others.

Another theological perspective that we need to address is the idea that we shouldn't worry or talk about possessions, that we should instead focus on "spiritual" matters and simply be content with whatever we have. This is a dangerous theological binary between what is material/embodied/secular and what is "spiritual." In progressive churches, we generally teach that our bodies are good and sacred, so much so that God became human in Jesus. We teach that injustice matters to God and is contrary to God's will. But we still often raise the spiritual above the material, the heavenly above the earthly. This dualism can make it hard to bring our spiritual values to bear on the earthly, practical matters such as buildings, salaries, and budgets. It can also harm people living in poverty—by telling people to be content with what they have, we are dismissing the real concerns of those who don't have enough and the oppressive structures that those who have enough or more than enough may be participating in and benefitting from. We need to integrate church finance and the rest of our material lives with our spirituality.

Our theological anthropology, the way we understand the role and nature of humans, also makes a difference to our understanding of just church finances. If we see humans, and by extension human institutions such as the church, as perfectly created by God, we will have difficulty critiquing church practices. If we see humans and our institutions as totally broken and inevitably sinful, we may have a hard time believing that positive change is possible at all, which will make it seem useless to try to make any changes. If we land somewhere in the middle, we might be able to both perceive injustice and believe addressing it is worthwhile—that what we have done is not perfect but that we must not simply throw up our hands, saying we will never get it right.

The concept of *koinonia* or community is another important theological concept with implications for our ethics. Sometimes we think of religion as a private, personal, individual matter. I've heard people say you can be a good Christian on your own, without being part of a community or a church. Focusing on *koinonia* challenges that idea and helps us to think of Christian identity as inherently communal. *Koinonia* is often spoken of as a form of radical community, transcending time and space, encompassing people who have died and who have not yet been born, all the world's peoples and maybe other creatures and parts of God's creation as well. If we believe we are called by God to participate in this sort of radical community, what church financial practices would show our kinship to all people in all places, to all parts of creation, in the past, present, and future?

If humans are flawed but not terminally broken, and yet radical community is essential to the practice of our faith, then we need to think about establishing right relations with one another—addressing sin and working to confess, repair, and repent. Sometimes in progressive churches we are hesitant to discuss sin, confession, and repentance. And that can be for good reason, given Christianity's tendency to focus on certain people and behaviors (often those related to sexuality). Many of these so-called sins (such as queer identities) are matters I and many others in progressive churches disagree are sinful to begin with. Ethicist Cynthia Moe-Lobeda emphasizes the need to consider structural and systemic sin, which are often overlooked in comparison to more personal or interpersonal sins.[3] Although we as individuals participate in systemic sin individually and do need to account for that, a systemic perspective reveals the complexity of our personal choices. It shifts the frame of these sins to reveal the roles played by social structures and institutions and shows the need to transform them.

A more systemic view of sin also reframes the concepts of confession and repentance, the acts of naming and making amends for injustice. In considerations of church finance, we can ask how systemic sin might be entwined with our practices. Are our financial practices embedded within systemic sin, or are they being put to use in service of our work toward repentance? For example, do our practices further racial wealth disparities, or are we using our church finances to redistribute wealth and make reparations? There is no "neutral" church financial arrangement that does neither, although it is possible that we might do both, for example, perhaps contributing to local reparations work while investing in ways that perpetuate injustice. Repentance sometimes conjures up images of harsh punishment or judgment, but the concept means to return, to turn back, or to restore. We can't go back in time, but we can strive to make amends for the past through practices like reparations and to move forward in more just ways.

Ecclesiology, our understanding of what it means to be the church, is another consideration for our ethical reflection. Different understandings of the nature and purpose of the church—our personal understandings and those prevalent in our faith community—lead to different approaches to church financial practices. For example, if the church is understood to exist primarily as a means to an end—to make disciples and convert people to Christianity, the "how" of church life (such as financial practices) may be viewed as relatively unimportant. Conceiving of the church as primarily a tool to foster community or even to develop individual awareness of social justice in the world may have similar implications. We might say that it doesn't matter how we structure or fund it as long as it gets the job done. On the other hand, if the church is understood to be a "foretaste" or anticipation of the coming kingdom (or as some prefer, kin-dom) of God, then the details of church life matter. In conversations about the church, the saying "actions speak louder than words" is often articulated as "practices preach." Our actions as church may serve to undermine or enhance our mission, even if the nature of the church itself is not viewed as theologically important. I find the idea of a foretaste of the reign of God (which I imagine as peace, justice, and flourishing for and among all people and all of creation) to be deeply evocative and compelling, even as I believe the church should also be a tool to enact justice in the wider world. My experiences of church as a community where the values I deeply believe in are lived out, at least sometimes, have helped to expand my imagination, sustain my spirit, and propel my hope for broader social change.

Christian History

Tradition is a mixed blessing as an ethical source, as there is much in the Christian tradition to both mourn and celebrate. An examination of tradition in our deliberations about just church finances can both restrict us, limiting our imaginations to what has been done before, and inspire us, upholding the values we hold dear and expanding our imaginations as we uncover possibly forgotten histories. The Acts community holding their possessions in common is a powerful witness to the possibilities for radical church finance and has inspired many Christian social experiments throughout history. Biblical scholar Richard Horsley describes the ancient Christian community at Qumran pooling their resources, and the early Christian community in Damascus, that created a form of community economic safety net.[4] The Damascans collected money to assist those who would otherwise have to go into debt to the oppressive powers of their day to meet their basic needs. Horsley asserts that these economic practices of the early church were an unprecedented example of horizontal wealth transfer among poor communities, rather than wealth being transferred hierarchically, primarily from poorer communities to richer ones.[5] He connects these ancient practices to the modern practices they inspired, such as Christian base communities in Latin America.[6] These base communities grew out of the Latin American liberation theology movement and involved small groups of mostly poor people coming together for worship and study, connecting the gospel to the circumstances of their lives and practices of mutual solidarity including sharing money and possessions with each other.

When I started university, I became involved with the Student Christian Movement, an ecumenical and justice-focused student organization. In its heyday, the 1940s to 1960s, an important program was summer "work camps" through which university students, at the time mostly from more privileged backgrounds, would spend summers working in lower-class settings such as factories. They would live in intentional communities with other work camp participants, pool their wages, study and reflect on the intersections of the gospel and the realities of workers, and at the end of the summer, distribute any remaining wages to the students most in need for the next school year. The stories about these work camps were powerful and inspiring and expanded my own imagination about what was possible. What would happen if churches provided opportunities for reflection on labor and the realities of workers? What might unfold if they engaged in struggles for labor justice, standing alongside marginalized workers, entering into relationship and solidarity? Perhaps members of the congregation or church community (for example, nursery-care providers, custodians, and so forth) could be invited to share honestly what their lives are like and what changes they would imagine both for themselves and others in similar roles. What might change if all of us viewed our earnings as not primarily our own and instead had challenging conversations about the needs among our community?

Church Statements

In most Christian denominations and many non-Christian faith traditions, people are thinking about economic justice. Through my involvement in denominations and the global ecumenical movement, I have had the privilege of attending gatherings where statements on various aspects of justice are crafted, debated, and carefully word-smithed. Although I often hear conversations about the politics of how these statements are written, who is involved in the process, and whether they have any impact on the world or the church, I do think that many of them offer a prophetic voice and vision. While none of them are perfect, their intention is worthy: to lift up and privilege marginalized voices, to call the church to live into its beliefs, and to decry injustice in both word and deed. Church statements can also be intended to help convince members that work for justice is in line with our traditions and necessitated by our faith. Statements from our own denominations and faith traditions can speak more directly to our own communities, while broader global and ecumenical statements can also be powerful because of their wide base of representation and uniting power for the church. I want to share two of those ecumenical statements: The World Council of Churches' (WCC) 2006 *AGAPE Call* and The World Alliance of Reformed Churches' (a predecessor organization of the current World Communion of Reformed Churches—WCRC) 2004 *Accra Confession.*

The Accra Confession was adopted at the 24th General Council meeting of the World Alliance of Reformed Churches in Accra, Ghana, in 2004.[7] An introduction to it states that "justice is a matter of faith."[8] Because economic and ecological justice are integral to Christian faith, it argues, the church must express solidarity with those who suffer (arising from the biblical traditions of both the prophets and Jesus's ministry), and it speaks movingly about how work for justice contributes to the unity of the church.[9] The Accra Confession is both a response to a specific call from the Southern African constituency of the church and to the general global situation of economic and ecological injustice. It describes the impacts of the present neoliberal economic system and then demonstrates the ways it is incompatible with Christian faith and is a manifestation of sin. It also critiques any theology that supports the idea that poverty is a result of individual fault.[10]

The World Council of Churches adopted their AGAPE (Alternative Globalization Affecting People and the Earth) statement at their 9th General Assembly in Porto Alegre, Brazil, in 2006. An introduction to the statement begins with the conviction that a "world without poverty is not only possible but is in keeping with the grace of God for the world."[11] Similar to the Accra Confession, the connection between theology/Christian faith and economic justice is emphasized. The statement arose out of a seven-year global study process that involved other global Christian organizations. AGAPE states that "we recognize that the divisions of the world are present among us" but that "we are called to be one in Christ . . . transformed by God's grace for the sake of all life on earth, overcoming the world's division."[12]

The statement identifies economic globalization and unfettered market forces as the primary origins of the present inequality and injustice in the world, among humans, and with the Earth.[13] It then notes that this global inequality is also present in the church and is incompatible with the call to be united in Christ.[14] Churches must be accountable to those impacted by economic injustice, meaning that privileged parts of the church must also be accountable to more oppressed parts, with their "first loyalty" to those experiencing injustice.[15] A background document to the AGAPE statement provides additional information, detailing the issues arising from the present economy but also providing more information about an "economy of life," which the statement presents as a hopeful alternative. Features of the "economy of life" include debt cancellation, ethical investment, and ecological justice.[16]

These statements, like many others, speak to the individual, societies, global systems, and the church. Global church organizations can provide an important window into the inequality present in the world, connecting Christians in wealthy countries with those in poorer settings, and can offer a profound opportunity to practice prioritizing the marginalized and redistributing resources, as well as to better understand the experiences of those with less power and how the global economy operates. Global and denominational settings can stretch our imaginations beyond the congregation as we consider what is possible and what our faith requires—being one in Christ, overcoming divisions, and living into a global community. Yet this community is marked by so much inequality that it can be hard to know where to begin changing our practices. Just because we feel uncertain about how to proceed and are unlikely to succeed entirely in this work does not mean that we should not enter into it and strive to do all we can. Prioritizing the voices, calls, and witness of those in the Global South can be one starting point, as we see demonstrated in these statements. We can learn about our denomination's budget and see how we can contribute to the needs of denominations and churches in the Global South. We can ask what their priorities are and work to ensure that the funds we offer are as unrestricted as possible and as stable and predictable year to year. We can develop relationships that challenge traditional donor–recipient power imbalances and seek to alleviate inequality at its root.

Intersectionality

The Bible, theology, Christian history, and church statements are essential resources for our deliberations on economic justice, but sources beyond those specific to the Christian tradition are also valuable. One such source is the concept of intersectionality, the term coined in 1989 by law professor Kimberlé Crenshaw. It arises from Black women's experiences, particularly those of struggle and oppression, and their resistance and analysis. Crenshaw drew on insights from a case where Black women's experiences were denied legal recognition and recourse in a case against General Motors because the law considered discrimination only based on gender *or* race but not both. Yet while Crenshaw is commonly credited for the concept, it was also developed in the work of other Black female scholars and also within many of the social movements of the 1960s and 1970s.[17]

Intersectionality looks at multiple social locations and identities working in concert in the lives of individuals, communities, cultures, institutions, nations, and more. It requires that we pay close attention to the ways power and privilege—and oppression and marginalization—operate. It emphasizes the multiple, complex faces of our identities, which exist within different systems where certain identities are valued more than others and are allowed more access to socially valued resources. Intersectionality underscores that we are never just one part of our identity. Our identities are multiple, shifting, mutually impacting, contextual, and sometimes contested.

Intersectional theory does not merely describe what is, however; it serves to create change toward greater justice. Yet, in many churches, when it comes to finance, people are primarily viewed from one perspective: the extent of their financial resources and their ability to give to the church. Intersectionality helps us to explore the ways our identities jointly impact our social relationships and personal circumstances. It reveals the many ways power and marginalization intersect with identities of both people and groups (such as churches). Privilege often manifests as greater access to financial resources and decision-making power, and holding multiple markers of privileged identities compounds that access; likewise, holding multiple markers of marginalization tends to multiply a person's financial hardship. When considering any financial arrangement or decision, it is essential to consider which identities, and therefore persons/communities, are likely to be privileged and marginalized. As we are committed to addressing inequality, we must center those who have been marginalized. If we bring an intersectional lens to our considerations of church finance, we will be compelled to rectify the inequality that exists in our churches and our world. We might value gifts of time, expertise, and skill alongside money. At the same time, realizing that some people are stretched for both time and money, and we might also encourage other people to give much more, so that some, in some circumstances, might primarily receive.

White Supremacy and Racial Justice

Although racial justice is an important component of intersectionality, in many privileged church contexts, white privilege and white supremacy require specific attention. Scholar and antiracism researcher Ibram X. Kendi is clear that there is no way to be "neutral" on the issue of racism: racists support "a racist policy through their actions of inaction or express a racist idea," while antiracists support "an antiracist policy through their actions or expressing an antiracist idea."[18] If we aren't actively engaged in antiracism, we are racist. There is no topic—including church finance and stewardship—that does not present an opportunity to either perpetuate racism or further antiracism. And this work is not only about the racial identities of the people in our churches. Even in churches with some racial diversity, white supremacy can be perpetuated by privileging whiteness in values, practices, and leadership. This bias can include not speaking openly and with nuanced understanding about issues related to money and inequality, but instead assuming that those who need financial assistance will ask for it (and in the "right" way) and approaching finance in an individualistic way, or assuming anyone can have enough if they just work hard and save.

Christian ethicist Karen Teel argues that white Christians have a particular responsibility to actively address race-based injustice due to white Christianity's culpability in creating and supporting many of the structures and ideologies that have led to historical and ongoing race-based inequalities and oppressive systems. White people are generally not aware of the advantages the system of white supremacy gives us, ranging from a greater likelihood of inheriting wealth to positive assumptions people make when they look at us, hear our voices, or read our names. White supremacy teaches those of us who are white to view successes as arising from personal merit and hard work and to assume the challenges of nonwhite/racialized people are the result of their individual shortcomings. We need to understand racism and white supremacy as systemic—operating through policies, institutions, histories, and ongoing realities that are much larger than individual people—rather than as expressions of only individual bias.

We also need to recognize that Christian practices can retrench white supremacy even when that might not be the intention behind these practices. Christian ethicist Traci West raises the example of intercessory prayers in which we who are white pray "for others" in a way that supports the notion that white people are not directly implicated in the situations we are praying for, so those praying do not need to change in any way. These prayers can put all the onus for action on God, giving those praying the feeling that progress will be made without their taking any action. They can also reinforce the image of white people as "saviors," who benevolently seek to help others, but who are not implicated within the situation or systemically culpable.[19] Additionally, when those of us who are white pray in thanksgiving to God for what we consider to be blessings in our lives, this can mask the role played by systems such as white supremacy and economic injustice in creating those privileges (which are perceived as blessings).[20] This masking is a particular concern with regard to finance in Christian contexts, as money is generally framed as a blessing and a gift from God. (Think about how we refer to money even in prayers of dedication or "invitations to the offering," which often begin with gratitude to God for money and resources.) Such a framing, as West's analysis identifies, may functionally imply that economic inequality is God's will and desire—that God is the cause of both wealth and poverty. As we know that economic inequality cuts along racial lines, this then suggests that God assents to, if not creates, racial injustice and inequality.

West also identifies that it is no accident that white supremacy and Christian theology are deeply entangled. She identifies the cultural fusion of Christian theology and European cultural biases and anti-Black racism throughout the two millennia of Christian history, expressed concretely in a number of brutal socioeconomic practices, including the transatlantic slave trade and the colonization of Black and brown peoples.[21] West also names the white racism that has been expressed within much of Christian mission engagement—that the spiritual and cultural traditions of many Black and brown communities are inadequate and the reason white missionaries have traveled for the purpose of Christian conversion.[22] Given these realities and others, the prospects for white Christians to adequately or even partially address racism and racial injustices are both urgent and challenging. Without directly and actively working against racism in its many manifestations, those of us who are white are being racist by our passivity, and we can continue to be racist even as we seek to work against racism in some ways. Theologian James Cone attests that although this work is a problematic and highly fraught enterprise, those of us who are white must work to align ourselves with Black peoples and enter into common cause and shared jeopardy through active solidarity.[23] A similar call applies to white communities in our relationships with all racialized communities. Although allyship is complex and will likely fall short of true Christian solidarity, striving for it is our only faithful option.

White supremacy and racial inequality are relevant to any discussion of finance, fundraising, and church practices. They directly and indirectly affect the money people have or do not have to contribute to their church, the reasons particular congregations or denominations have greater or lesser wealth, which churches people attend and how people are received and perceived in those communities, how people understand and relate to money either as individuals/families or as a church community, and many other factors. Additionally, considerations of white privilege are relevant to church mission and financial support, including which churches or individuals are perceived as, or are in fact, givers or recipients. Who has power in decision-making? Does a white person's membership in a predominantly white church further entrench their white privilege by offering, for example, social and business connections? Is your head spinning yet? Becoming aware of the impact of white supremacy and racial injustice on our money can certainly complicate church finance. But we cannot do our work for justice in an integrated way without that awareness.

Decolonial Practice

Decoloniality—challenging the forces and legacies of colonialism—is another framework for viewing justice and church finances. Many Christian churches have worked to repudiate the Doctrine of Discovery—a legal concept that originated in Europe in the fifteenth century with a papal bull and has been used by many countries, including in the United States as recently as 2005, to justify the colonization and seizure of lands inhabited by non-Christians— and to make amends for our participation in numerous colonial projects. Decolonial theory considers all social relations in the context of colonial projects and neocolonial realities. Guatemalan Canadian ethicist Néstor Medina argues it can help us to detect and uncover "the hidden colonial web of relations governing our inherited intellectual configuration and modernist Eurocentric understandings of knowledge, ethnocultural identity, world history, racial background, and religious traditions."[24] In the North American context,[25] decolonial analysis reveals the structures through which power, land, and resources have been stolen by European settler-colonizers. This analysis is essential to church contexts because churches themselves were active participants in these colonial projects, both practically and ideologically.

Any consideration of economic justice must acknowledge that the wealth of many European descendants in North America has been amassed through colonial endeavors both within North America itself (such as through resource extraction and land seizure) and globally (such as through global trade and business). Decoloniality shows that "the entire social, political, economic, and cultural structures of modernity are predicated on imposed relations of domination."[26] Indigenous worldviews tend to emphasize the centrality of land and place, in contrast to European/Western perspectives that tend to be more oriented around a linear understanding of time, history, and development.[27] A decolonized, place-focused perspective emphasizes that people hold ethical responsibilities not only toward other people but also to particular places, including land, animals, and plants.[28]

This analysis looks beyond power relations between people. A focus on dispossession and exploitation of land and creatures also reveals the way wealth in North America, including in North American churches, has been amassed through colonization. An awareness of these realities must impact our understanding of church finance. It should cause us to question what we understand to be ours and to examine the land where we are located and its Indigenous history. We should enter into relationship with local Indigenous communities and begin to make amends for the past and engage in campaigns and coalitions based in principles of solidarity to work for a better future.

Environmental and Climate Justice

The Earth itself is an ethical source. The climate crisis poses a pressing existential threat to humanity, other species, and to the ecological systems that sustain us all. And climate change does not affect all people or all bioregions similarly, nor are all people equally culpable. It is yet another privilege-reinforcer, hardest on those already on the margins, less so for those of us who are already privileged. For this reason, the movement for environmental justice analyzes the intersections of social (in)justice, ecological devastation, and climate change. It seeks to rectify the ways the mainstream environmental movement often ignores issues of social justice. Rather than universalizing, environmental justice focuses on particular communities, experiences, and identities. Who has contributed most to climate change, who is most impacted by it, and how we must focus on the experiences of those who are most marginalized?

Christian churches have contributed to climate change and climate injustice by espousing dualities and hierarchies between the spiritual and the material, heaven and earth, humans and nonhuman parts of creation. Historian Lynn White gave a foundational speech on Christianity's contribution to environmental degradation in 1966 (published in 1967), entitled "The Historical Roots of Our Ecologic Crisis." He argued that humanity's view of the natural world as simply a resource for human consumption finds its roots within Christianity. Specifically, he named Christians' interpretation of humanity's "dominion" over the rest of the natural world and the notion that humans are superior to other animals because humans have a soul and the ability to reason.[29] Much work has been done to challenge these views and reinterpret this concept of dominion, including Pope Francis's encyclical *Laudato si'*, which emphasizes human responsibility and care for creation.

In matters of church finance, Christians and churches have contributed to social injustice and environmental devastation and the intersecting of the two, and we have ethical responsibilities to address these realities and to act differently now and into the future. We have often contributed to climate change directly through our property management practices, such as using fossil fuels to power our buildings and investing money in companies that contribute to the climate crisis. We travel in individual cars (or even by plane) to attend church services, programs, conferences, and meetings; use disposable, single-use food-service items; and landscape our properties in water-intensive ways unsuited to our bioregions. Sometimes, we do not pursue more ecologically sound projects (for example, installing solar panels) due to their cost and our failure to prioritize actions to mitigate climate change. In our teaching and preaching, we have not paid adequate attention, either explicitly or implicitly, to values that support environmental justice such as simplicity, sufficiency, and sustainability. How might our church finance practices be different if addressing environmental injustice is a central and guiding commitment?

Sources for You and Your Community

Which of the concepts, values, and stories offered in this chapter resonated with you? Which made you the most

uncomfortable? Which ideas, communities, and commitments do you feel most called to learn more about
and to integrate into your church's practices? To practice
social justice through church finances, we first need to
name and examine the forces that have shaped us and our
communities—for good and for ill. We need to be aware
of our own and others' struggles for justice, work going on
in our churches, throughout our communities, and around
the world. We need to make connections between topics
that might not immediately seem to be related to each
other, recognizing that ideas will be most compelling when
they are connected to matters we already care about. What
resonates will vary in different settings. In some contexts, a
denominational statement will hold a lot of weight, while,
in others, such a document will be off-putting and lead
to skepticism among people who might otherwise be on
board. The good news is that the foundations for a commitment to justice abound both within and outside Christian
tradition. Based on these foundations, we can connect to
stories, communities, and individuals who can support,
sustain, and challenge us in this work. Those of us from
privileged backgrounds need to foster relationships and
involvements that will challenge our thinking and deepen
our understandings of justice, so we aren't working alone
or only with others of similar experiences. Exploring the
perspectives of those who have experienced injustice, and
doing so alongside and in active dialogue with them, will
sharpen our analysis and ensure we are partnering with, not
usurping the agency of, those communities.

In this chapter, we rooted ourselves in some of the
important components of our faith tradition (scripture,

Christian theology, tradition, global church statements) and ethical commitments (intersectionality, racial justice, decoloniality, and environmental justice) that we want to inform our lives and our churches—especially our church financial practices. In the next chapter we will consider our practices themselves. What values do they embody? What forces and values have shaped them? What do we learn if we view them through the perspectives of privilege and marginalization, individualism, and radical community? How can we unmask the injustice underlying practices, so they no longer seem natural or neutral? As we dive into the next chapter, I invite you compare your social justice values to your financial practices and to notice if familiar church practices begin to seem "strange" to you. Anthropology can be described as a task of making what has been familiar strange, and the strange familiar. Critical engagement with theology and justice can do the same. Sometimes getting some distance from our usual practices can help us to see the values embedded with them and to imagine alternatives that might not typically come to mind. I hope that this is already beginning to happen for you and will continue as we go on.

2.

The Gods of the Market

Exposing the Idols of Neoliberalism

Now that we've looked at the values that should inform us as we engage in church finance, let's look at the values underlying our current practices. You might already be thinking about the disconnects you have experienced between some of the ideals explored in chapter 1 and the everyday realities of church life. I've served in various leadership roles in multiple church communities, so I am aware of how difficult it can be to address the divide between what we say we believe and what we do. I also know there are many complex reasons churches—and church leaders—do things the way they do.

If you're saying to yourself, "But wait, my church is different," please know I believe you might be right! Churches are different from each other. I also hope it's clear I have been caught up in many of the perspectives I criticize, so I am not critiquing from "on high." I fall short of my ideals all the time. But I still think it is worthwhile to look at what is going on in the world of Christian stewardship and to think about what it all means. If you have been sensing some discomfort about what you are doing, this chapter might help to identify some of your concerns.

The values embedded in church financial practices are common in the broader world of finance and fundraising, which is itself rooted in our neoliberal capitalist economy, entwined with Eurocentric values and assumptions. Scholar David Harvey defines neoliberalism as an intensified form of capitalism that emerged in the 1970s and became dominant in many countries, including the United States, in the 1990s. It is based on the idea that free markets are necessary to ensure personal freedom and that the best role for the state (or the government) is to help the market by reducing regulations, taxes, and social services.[1] The state's job is to protect private property and to make it easier for businesses to make profits.[2] This economic system is deeply entangled with white supremacy and other oppressive systems (such as patriarchy, ableism, and colonialism), which define whose interests are prioritized and who is seen as a threat to maximizing profits as well as what values are present. Proponents believe charities, families, and individuals should provide many of the services that might be offered by the government in a different economic system, such as care for children and the elderly, education, health care, and support for the economically marginalized.

Underlying values and assumptions—that making the most money is everyone's goal, that individual and organizational freedoms are primary goods, and that we have little responsibility toward those who struggle—run deep and cannot be separated from the systems they are embedded within. Despite these problematic values, you might be thinking, when churches talk about money, they are usually just trying to raise enough money to stay open—and besides, we do a lot to help out our communities. But when we let these values define our fundraising and financial practices, then it is these values and the systems they are connected to, rather than the values of our faith, that are shaping us, as individuals and as churches. For example, many churches assume we should try our best to increase our revenue without really deeply examining why. Most assume that it is our responsibility to try to keep our church open and that we fail if we can't. We also think that, if we are doing okay, it is not really our problem if other people or other churches are deeply struggling.

At the same time, as churches we have established some ethical boundaries when it comes to raising money; the ends don't justify all the means. We already say we wouldn't charge a fee to sit in the best seats at church, rent out our hall to a neo-Nazi militia group, or expect payment from those who meet to pray with the pastor. And many denominations and congregations have made commitments to avoid investing in alcohol, tobacco, or firearms. So how do we take the next step to go deeper, looking at more of our ethical commitments and using those to reexamine our goals and methods?

What Is Christian Stewardship?

The word *stewardship* gets thrown around a lot when discussing church finance. Biblical scholar and theologian Mark Allan Powell observes that many Christians think of stewardship as synonymous with fundraising, but it is a broader concept that recognizes God as the ultimate authority over our lives and our possessions—in fact, over the whole world.[3] So, yes, stewardship is about church financial practices, but it is also about God's sovereignty and human responsibility. It undergirds a Christian perspective on environmentalism—the idea that people are stewards of a creation that ultimately belongs to God, and that the world is more than just a resource for us to use and discard as we please. While this is a powerful idea for some people, others argue that it still maintains the idea that humans are separate from and superior to the rest of the natural world.

This isn't a book about Christian environmentalism, of course—but the notion of stewardship of creation gives us some insight into stewardship of our finances. In both arenas, the concept of stewardship encourages us to ask who is in charge. Who "owns" what? Do we? Or does the Earth, money, the church itself, and everything else belong to God? Seeing our money as ours to do with as we please might mean we don't have much of an obligation to use it to serve God or the community. Even if we think "our" money is ultimately God's, we still might wonder what that means on a practical level. Do we need to give some portion of it to the church? If God gave us whatever money we have, be it a huge amount or not enough to survive, do we need to—or get to—ask questions about fairness or justice?

If we are called to be stewards of the church, does that mean God created churches as they are, and we shouldn't make too many changes—just keep them in good working order the best we can until we can give them back to God? Some books about stewardship use the image of a steward as a house-sitter. When I am house-sitting, I know it isn't my place to make any major changes to the home. I'm just supposed to keep everything safe and in good order until the property owner comes back. If this is how we think of our role in our churches, does the idea limit our imaginations and quell our motivation and our ability to take radical steps for justice? Is that compatible with, say, returning the property (in whole or part) to the Indigenous community on whose territory we are located and whose colonization we may have participated in?

Twelve Idols in Christian Stewardship

Stewardship might serve us as a useful metaphor for how we take care of our money, our churches, and the Earth. It can be a helpful reminder of God's active presence in and through all the world, the church included. But we need to be mindful of the ways it might limit us or steer us away from more just action or radical change. We need to examine the specific values and beliefs informing our understanding and action.

Through my study of books related to Christian stewardship and church finance, interviews with pastors and church leaders, and case studies I conducted, I have identified twelve values and beliefs (idols) that underlie many Christians' stewardship practices. These are rooted in aspects of neoliberalism (and its related systems), rather than to the ethical commitments I wrote about in chapter 1. I call them "idols" because they are both cherished and false. They underpin many of our mainstream practices and are incompatible with our beliefs. Many of them are so common they might not seem notable to you right away. But I hope in reflecting on these twelve idols—predominant values and beliefs—you can see how they might limit our churches and prevent our pursuit of important values that arise from our faith, such as justice, equality, redistribution, reconciliation, and sustainability.

What's Mine Is Mine

The idea that what is in my possession, "my property," belongs to me and that I can use it however I please is so fundamental in our society that we have difficulty even considering an alternative. Proponents of neoliberalism assume everyone has the freedom to earn as much money as they want and that it is fine to have more than we need as long as we didn't obtain it through illegal or unquestionably immoral means. Those who don't have enough—well, we think, that's too bad, but their situation isn't connected to what we have or how we came to obtain it. While we think giving away some of what we have is admirable, we also think we may choose not to give anything away and still be a morally okay person or church. If we give a little something, we can pat ourselves on the back. After all, lots of people and churches don't give anything away at all.

We need to ask, What is actually "mine"? We need to ask where our "property" originates and who has been harmed all along the way as it has come into our lives. When I look at my life and my personal finances, I realize how much of what I have is the result of white privilege, my privileged socioeconomic class, my life in the Global North, and devastating processes that are impacting other people and species, the Earth, and future generations. Social and practical forms of privilege allowed me to pursue higher education and to believe, behave, and expect to be treated as though I belonged in that environment. Many of us have benefitted from low-price goods made possible by paying some workers, particularly people in the Global South, less than living wages—and at a great cost to the planet. If we recognize the means through which we have obtained what we have and ask whether it is ethically acceptable to have more than enough when others have far less than enough and the planet is suffering immensely (with climate change also causing further human suffering), claiming that what we have is simply "ours" seems suspect.

When we examine churches' assets, the situation is similarly complex. While we commonly say, "Well, people gave us this money, and now it's ours to do with as we (alone) discern," we are oversimplifying, ignoring the people and places impacted by the creation of the funds and the ways privilege and injustice determined who had money to give (and who did not). If our church financial assets have been given by members who are individually and collectively entwined in systems that privilege them (and marginalize others), our collective ethical responsibility must also take that into account. If as a church we have investments even in so-called ethical funds that may still profit in some ways from exploiting people and the planet, we need to expand our criteria for what "ethical" means. If we live and build churches on traditional Indigenous territory and in gentrified or predominantly white communities, we profit and benefit from the land, its location, and these systems. We need to uncover how colonial and racist systems of migration and neighborhood development have enhanced the value of our property. We also need to be aware that churches with money and privilege often grow and attract more privileged members due to their facilities, staffing, programming, advertising, location, and other factors not available to other church communities.

In considerations of church finance, however, we often act as though our churches and their money exist in a vacuum—separate from other churches and systemic factors. While we might not be willing to receive a plate offering from someone we know had stolen the money, invest our church resources in a tobacco company, or earn rental income from an LGBTQ+ "conversion therapy" organization, our ethical responsibilities mean all those impacted by our bank account—and the history of those funds—need to be included at the table, literally (through who is present in our decision-making conversations) and metaphorically (through what we take into account as we discern).

Giving Is Generous

We generally assume making a donation of any amount is a positive voluntary action. Just think of the phrase "Thank you for your generosity!" How often have you said or heard something like that? Why would we ever criticize it? Shouldn't we praise and acknowledge people who give? After all, they didn't have to! But once we discover the problem with "what's mine is mine," we start to see the problem with praising generosity. If what we have isn't truly "ours" to use in whatever way we want, then giving isn't simply an optional and generous choice. It's an ethical requirement. This requires us to rethink the way we understand giving.

Because of privilege, I've had resources to give, and I've felt the warmth of a "thank you, that's so generous" many times myself. It's a social convention acknowledging that I made a decision to give. But embedded in that praise and thanks is the assumption that I didn't *have* to give (and that the amount I gave, however small, was acceptable). In a practical sense, and as our society currently operates, that is absolutely true. But when I think about my commitments and what I believe, I see that giving is essential, an obligation rather than an option. Giving away some of what I have is part of acknowledging that I don't deserve to have more than others, and certainly not to the extremes that currently exist in our world. It is tied to reparations, redistribution, and my deep belief that the suffering of humanity and the Earth is something I must strive to address with the resources I have. Because I believe all people should have what they need—like I do—sharing resources isn't simply a nice thing I can choose to do if I want to or feel like it.

Churches giving some of their funds to local or global organizations and church partners is also often framed as a generous act. But again we must ask, can we truly justify having so much more than others? The concept of generosity can distract us from our deep moral obligations to one another and limit our ability to discuss how much is actually appropriate. The term "generosity" may still have a place in our stewardship practices, but we need to ask how it may lead us to think of giving as good but optional, rather than intrinsic to our ethical obligations to one another in an unjust world.

More Is Better!

We tend to believe more is better than less, especially with regard to money and property. But is more *always* better? How much is enough? We live in a society where power is associated with factors such as size, growth, and reach. As individuals, we are told both explicitly and implicitly to earn as much money as we can, and we view people who have earned a lot as highly successful and to be admired and emulated. The same is true for organizations: the bigger the better. We assume the market rewards those with innovative ideas and meaningful missions with ample resources, devoted followers, and increasing memberships. But as we have already discussed, many systemic factors also contribute to how much we—as individuals and communities—have.

In our churches, we tend to operate as if more is better. We don't stop to ask whether a church can have enough (or even too much) money. On one hand, the reasons cited for wanting more often seem good. Most churches can dream up a list of what they'd do with more money in no time. We want to be able to serve the community more, expand programming, pay fair salaries—and sometimes just keep our doors open. But while our list might be justifiable and even do good in many cases, there are other factors to reflect on. Sometimes we duplicate programming that already exists in the community or strive to offer social services that we aren't really equipped and trained to provide (including things that might be more appropriately accomplished by government). Asking people to give as much as they can to the church might even mean they have less to devote to other worthy causes. We need to not assume that more programs, more services, more staff, more property are inherently better.

Another aspect of the belief that more is better is thinking smaller things don't matter, or at least don't matter much. This may mislead us to think that smaller churches, or those with smaller budgets, are inherently inferior. While we need to carefully consider the factors that might lead some churches to be smaller or have fewer resources (for example, systemic inequality), we also need to consider the gifts of smaller communities (for example, intimacy) or those that choose a smaller budget and simpler format. With respect to individual contributions and gifts to church, the assumption that more is better might also lead us to think smaller contributions don't make a difference. We can remember Jesus praising the widow who gave two coins and receive this as an invitation to think differently about what gifts, and which givers, matter. We shouldn't pressure people to give beyond their means or even insist that everyone must give something, even during times when they are struggling deeply. Rather, we should take into account circumstances and intention, and challenge the assumption that smaller things matter less.

Many forces, from our economic system to our educational system, reinforce the idea that more must be better. Resisting this assumption means aiming for "enough" instead of "as much as possible," striving for adequacy and sufficiency in our church budgets and in our own lives. We should evaluate our own needs and desires alongside the needs of individuals, other organizations, and society at large. We should question the idea that churches need to compete (and, ideally, "win!") in the marketplace of charities and causes to ensure we get as much of the donation pot as we can for ourselves. We should acknowledge that causes other than church are important, that organizations other than churches often do the very work we feel our faith calls us to participate in, such as pursuing equity in society and protecting the most vulnerable human communities and ecosystems. We should also recognize that people struggle to determine how much to give to different organizations and how much to keep for themselves and their families (especially given the amount of economic uncertainty faced by so many). As church leaders, we should gladly engage in careful discernment about these different needs and help church members to do the same, rather than just repeatedly asking people to give, and give more.

As we reshape our individual and collective vision for a more just world, we glimpse a world beyond the pressure of constant growth and accumulation. What other goals might we find are possible? Sufficiency, adequacy, sustainability, ethical alignment, justice, creativity, right relations, and faithfulness are others that come to mind for me. As Christians and as churches, the goal of faithfulness to the gospel is particularly pertinent. We might feel as though we are failing when we look to our past glories when our Sunday schools were bursting, or when we look to other churches that seem materially and financially successful. But if growth is no longer a goal or even a good, we might be freed to do and to be more faithful and impactful than we ever imagined.

We're All the Same

Many of us believe that, ultimately, people are more similar to one another than we are different, and so in most cases we can speak to all people with one message. The idea that we're all basically the same (at least in an economic sense) is rooted in a neoliberal and white supremacist view that each individual is a free agent, able to earn as much as the next person if they just work hard. While we are all equal in our value and worth as humans, deep inequalities exist in our world. Identity factors (such as age, race, nationality, gender, and sexuality) and systems of power affect one's access to resources and, in that way, we are not the same at all. On a broader level, we know that neighborhoods (and churches) are often stratified by factors such as race and class, for example.

In our practices of Christian stewardship, we often give the same message to people regardless of their different financial circumstances. Although some of our churches might not be as diverse as we'd like, or even that we might imagine exists, there is at least some difference in financial situations. A universal message can be harmful to those who are economically marginalized, at best making them feel unwelcome in church and at worst causing harm. Stewardship campaigns often encourage proportional giving—the idea that rather than giving the same amount, people should give the same percentage of their salary as a way to take class and economic differences into consideration. But given how extreme inequality is, proportional giving does not take into account the differing levels of sacrifice the same percentage of income might represent for a poor person than for a rich person.

Many people who write about stewardship seem to believe that most (or even all) people are not giving as much as they could, so authors tend to emphasize the need for larger and more sacrificial gifts. They don't consider how those messages would strike someone on a tight budget, someone who might come to believe the church is yet another place that doesn't understand or care about those living in poverty, just another place more concerned with sustaining itself than with helping people thrive despite our world's broken systems. Authors writing about stewardship tend to be quite dismissive of people's feelings of financial vulnerability and their hesitancy to give. But in many cases, people's fears about finances are real and legitimate. Even those of us who are getting by right now know that losing a job or an unexpected bill can be the start of a difficult cycle of poverty. And even those of us with access to plenty of money know that the social safety net is minimal and that not all of us have family and friends to turn to when times are difficult, especially in a social climate that prizes self-sufficiency. In progressive churches, we say that people's embodied and material realities matter and that all people should have enough. We say no one should live in fear of scarcity. When all of our steward-ship messaging says simply that people should give, and give more, we undermine the idea that we truly care that all should have enough.

Thinking about how those who are struggling in our congregations will hear stewardship messages doesn't mean we have to stop encouraging giving. But we need to challenge the notion that we're all the same and par-ticularly attend to the experiences of members who are marginalized in any ways. To do this, we must consult with and include in financial leadership these people. In some cases, different emphases and messages might be appropriate for different members. Our practices should challenge rather than entrench ideologies of economic injustice. If we acknowledge and support those who are stressed about their finances and help them to feel (and truly be) less alone in their struggles, we will truly be bringing our faith into our stewardship practices.

Greed (Is All That) Impedes Giving

Another common assumption that shapes our financial practices is that the primary, if not only, reason people don't give more to their church is that they are greedy— that people want to keep whatever money they have for themselves, primarily to spend on luxuries they don't really need. So the primary message of a lot of Christian steward- ship material in response is that greed is bad and generos- ity is good. And of course, like many of the other values I'm unpacking, it's not entirely wrong, at least not on the surface. Many people in churches (myself included) have more money than is required to keep them alive or even comfortable. But an emphasis on greed can actually hide the deep reasons people might be reticent to give more.

In our present economy, not having enough money can be a matter of life and death. Even if we are financially com- fortable in the present, we know that jobs can be lost and crises can arise. One of the primary features of employment in our present economy is precariousness. Increasingly, people work in jobs where pay varies; we don't know how many shifts we will get or how long any given job will last. Increasingly, people piece together an income from various sources. Gig workers and those in more informal work arrangements know this fluctuation all too well. How can we make an annual pledge to our church when we don't know how much we will have week to week, let alone year to year?

Uncertain earnings make budgeting difficult, as does the expense side of the ledger. The cost of housing, childcare, education, health care, and senior care can be substantial and variable. Even seemingly simple solutions, such as cutting nonessentials, can be complex and result in hidden costs. Much so-called luxury spending is social. A friend invites us to go on a group trip, our child begs to join a team with their friends, a colleague posts about an urgent need on a crowd-funding website, we want to support the fair-trade business or the organic farm—all may be worthy expenditures. Also, we often make financial decisions as part of couples and families (and, increasingly, spouses and partners do not share the same faith practices or religious traditions), in networks of friends, immersed within institutions, cultures, and systems much larger than us. To live within our means, as we are often told we must, is not simple. Often in Christian stewardship, we are imagined to be autonomous individuals in control of all the factors that affect our financial lives. It is not that greed is never a factor, but it is far from the only or even primary reason people don't give more.

Scarcity Is Just a Poor Attitude

Another common assumption is that people who are reticent to give more money to church (irrationally) fear scarcity, an attitude that shows a lack of faith in God. Stewardship leaders encourage people to trust that material abundance will be given to them, perhaps even as a reward for their giving to the church. The concepts of scarcity and abundance often arise in stewardship campaigns and especially in preaching and messages about giving. But rather than examining the complex reasons leading to inequality, why some people have too much and many too little, we assume scarcity and abundance are merely mindsets a person or church chooses and that because more is better, we should simply choose to believe in abundance.

Whether we experience material scarcity or abundance, sometimes our perceptions do not line up with reality. Congregational leaders often form two camps—those who always want to save as much money as possible for leaner times (scarcity) and those who want to give away resources to organizations doing good work in the community or spend money on new initiatives (abundance). Generally speaking, those who want to save understand that their responsibility is to ensure the future of the church, while those who want to spend understand that giving away or spending resources is essential to being the church now and that resources will be provided when they are needed. Those who want to save more worry about declining membership and think the prudent thing to do is to build up a cushion. Those who want to spend think creating a cushion turns people off from church and that engaging in the community attracts people. Those who want to save think an attitude of abundance is naive and irresponsible, and those who want to spend dismiss the fear of scarcity as unfaithful.

In my experience, these differing orientations toward scarcity (saving) and abundance (spending or giving) are significant sources of underlying frustration and conflict, especially among church leaders, but are not generally discussed openly. So much of our decision-making arises from formational life experiences and long-time habits—and dismissing or minimizing fears such as scarcity doesn't do them justice, particularly when people are experiencing such scarcity. We need to identify our default attitudes toward resources, explore where these attitudes come from, and carefully evaluate what resources—risks and abundance—are really on the table—for us, for others, for the church, and for the planet.

The Donor Is Always Right

Most leaders of organizations that depend on donors try to keep them happy, even if that means acquiescing to demands or desires we may disagree with. The "donor is always right" attitude is rooted in the notion that "what's mine is mine": if resources belong to the giver, we should follow the giver's wishes as much as possible. Of course, as church leaders, we want to serve people and to honor different people's voices and perspectives. And because we live in a customer service–oriented culture, people with financial means are accustomed to being catered to and listened to. In some cases, letting the donor have extra influence seems like a small concession; they are supporting the organization, after all. And pragmatically, we assume this approach raises more money (and more is better, right?). If increasing donations is our primary goal, why wouldn't we want to get to know our donors and develop a project that will match their interests, perhaps motivating them to give more than they would to a general fund? If a few major contributors to our church aren't happy with the overall direction, perhaps it's just practical for us to pivot. Sometimes there is a strategic reason to bend to donors' voices, of course. But doing so can be ethically problematic. It might mean we are letting those who are economically (and often in other ways) privileged have a greater voice. It might mean we pursue agendas that don't align with priorities we've collectively discerned or that are not truly faithful.

One church I've known loves to conduct surveys. One study about the children's program suggested that some people wanted it to primarily teach Bible stories, and others wanted a program focused on humanistic values, such as kindness and community, without references to faith. Congregational leaders didn't want to lose any members—or any givers—so they decided the best strategy would be to create two distinct programs, one that took each approach. No one paused to ask whether more complex issues were at play (such as whether hesitancy about Bible stories might arise from concern about biblical literalism) or whether there were certain limits that we should not cross if we were not to lose our identity as a church. Leaders at this church dealt with every survey they conducted by trying to meet every desire and keep every person happy. In fact, that was the foundation of their understanding of what the church should be: whatever people asked for. Of course, we want to get people's input and to be a participatory and evolving community, but we need to be faithful first to our values and identity. We need to be willing to take risks for the sake of who we are called to be as the church, even if our decisions might cause some people to leave or some givers to close their wallets.

Donor-Directed, Program-Specific Giving Options Are Best

A practice related to the belief that the donor is always right can be seen in the trend to allow donors to direct their funds, and to separate out "programs" from "core" or "administrative" funds in organizational budgets. This separation, in part, allows donors to feel their money is having more of an impact because it directly supports programmatic work. I'm sure we've all seen advertisements for charities that tell us that a $5 gift will buy someone one meal and $50 will provide someone shelter for a night. Many of us have looked through an organization's "giving catalogue" to choose which project most sparks our imagination or is the best fit for our friend's birthday. In a way this strategy makes sense. It helps us to picture what our donation will do and assures us our gift aligns with our own priorities or will seem special to the person it is honoring. But quantifiable types of work are easy to promote in this way, while less tangible needs become much harder to fund. (How do we quantify advocacy work? "Five dollars buys ___"?) Organizations that receive designated donations often feel the need to minimize "overhead," to the point that staff are not paid a living wage and infrastructure becomes severely outdated. Projects and organizations compete with one another to provide the most cost-effective and most attractive (to donors) projects.

A campus ministry organization I worked with was once invited to be profiled in a denominational giving catalogue from which people could choose ministries to support. It was hard to come up with the right tangible gift idea—$20 will buy coffee and muffins for a small group meeting?—because most of our income was used to pay a staff person to organize programs. Seeing our ministry listed next to one inviting people to give $20 to buy a drinking well for a rural village in the Global South felt awkward and forced a sense of competition. Previously, these denominational ministries had primarily been supported through a large pool of funds that provided annual grants (largely consistent each year, allowing for long-range planning) that could be used for whatever the organization determined was best. Careful ethical discernment was done by a diverse body of elected church leaders about how to balance different types of organizations, both local and global. The giving catalogue was created to deal with a funding shortfall and to encourage people to support these ministries, rather than give a physical gift or use a gift catalogue from a different nonprofit organization. But these catalogues, which operate under free-market principles, give donors a lot of power to determine what organizations and projects get supported. Groups might shift what they do to appeal to donors. And when donors are predominantly white people in the Global North, such catalogues permit wealthy white people to determine priorities for the whole world. Organizations might welcome designated or program-specific donations, especially if they will in the end receive more support than they might otherwise. But recipients' voices, not donors' desires, should be at the center of this process.

Bequests can be especially difficult, because sometimes money is given for and then tied to a specific purpose that might not even exist in the future. We need to think carefully about how much time and energy we are spending on major givers (and therefore not on other community members) and the extent to which their contributions give them power. Many of us know of churches that have not taken stands on same-sex marriage or publicly supported the Black Lives Matter movement because they fear it might cause the biggest givers to hold back. But we need not assume donors will insist on being catered to and there's nothing we can do about it. Some people with privilege and means might be willing to give an unrestricted gift if they understand that this would allow the congregation as a whole to determine priorities, now and in the future. It's critical that we carefully evaluate the sway that donors—people with various forms of privilege—have over the ministries of our churches and the call of our faith.

The Wealthy and Privileged Should Be in Charge

We sometimes assume the people in financial leadership in a church should be those who have contributed the most. This approach is generally endorsed for a variety of reasons, such as: these people are highly invested in the life of the church; they may know how to encourage others to give at a high level; they have had personal success with money; and giving them a leadership role will help them to continue to feel invested in the life of the church and want to keep giving. Much of the guidance about stewardship (and fundraising more generally) says that those in leadership should be top givers. Some even root this principle in Paul's image of the body of Christ—one body with many parts, wealth being a sort of "spiritual gift" given by God to some and not to others. This is theologically problematic, of course, given the systemic and structural reasons some people have a great deal more than others.

Not only church folk believe those with lots of money (who we know are more likely to be white, male, straight, able-bodied, and so on) should be our teachers and leaders on matters of money. Wealthy and privileged people are heads of banks and government agencies, not just church stewardship and finance ministries. Advice about investing and giving means nothing if we have little or nothing to invest or give. On the other hand, we might learn about simple and creative ways to live from those who've been able to manage on a limited budget. Neoliberalism and white supremacy falsely tell us that the people with money have achieved their status through merit alone. When church leaders and teachers are all people with economic means, we replicate and further the world's hierarchies of privilege and marginalization. We miss out on the wisdom, perspectives, and priorities of those who have experienced oppression and who might lead us to a more countercultural approach to finance.

We Must Share Only Good News

In Christian stewardship and fundraising circles, one of the strategies often shared is to stay positive, regardless of what is going on. "No one wants to give to a sinking ship!" Hope and trust in the goodness of God's promises for the future are important, but they do not supplant the need to be (at least mostly) honest about a situation. An exclusive focus on the positive, despite the reality, is rooted in the assumption that more is better, so we must spin the facts to reflect success or growth, and minimize or mask information about decline or shortfalls. This leads to superficial community engagement, rather than honest wrestling with complex realities and difficult emotions. Theologically and pastorally, there is much to be gained by naming and living into lament, anxiety, frustration, and uncertainty. We allow a community to grapple together with a challenging situation, rather than manipulating them to feel good so they will want to give.

An emphasis on positivity is in part intended to avoid using fear as a motivator—"If you all don't open your wallets today, our church is going to close!" Stewardship consultants also want to avoid talking about the matter only in times of need, moving from crisis to crisis—"The roof is leaking! The organ needs repair! We are behind on our budget projection!"—until people just tune it all out. But access to information is power. When our stewardship messages are too carefully scripted to focus on the positive, regardless of the reality, we create an "in group" (those in the know, often the ones crafting the message) and an "out group" (those who hear only the message that has been crafted for them and who do not know what is really going on). Those who are in the "out group" also can't be involved in a meaningful way in creating solutions to financial problems.

Telling the truth about financial challenges is also important on a practical level. For example, people who have been told the truth, who trust we are telling the truth about this and other matters, are not surprised when serious challenges become unavoidable. "What do you mean, we need to make huge cuts? All you've ever said was thank you for your generosity!" Truth telling is also essential to talking about difficult things and inviting others to offer their ideas and support. We can't fully address problems that aren't fully named.

For many years the United Church of Canada's denominational magazine featured bright, positive stewardship ads that would say how many millions had been raised for the denomination in the previous year. The ads had a celebratory feel and, of course, they said "thank you!" What they didn't say was that the denominational leaders deliberately set the goal amount lower each year. So, although the stated "goal" had been reached, it wasn't enough money to sustain the previous level of work. This created a real sense of confusion and disconnect when staff and budgets were inevitably cut. It was hard for those of us who were concerned to organize against these cuts or to do any kind of grassroots fundraising campaigns to support the denomination because most people had no idea there was a problem. Leaders believed people would not want to give to a "failing" or a "dying" institution and that they therefore had to offer a positive message. But to have a real conversation about finances, we all need accurate information— negative and positive. If we're told only that we're meeting our goals and everything is going great, we might not feel our contribution matters much (and might give elsewhere instead). Complete information isn't a guarantee that a budget will be met, of course, but knowing a worthy cause is likely to face a shortfall can lead to tremendous creativity in collective efforts to prevent it. And if the goal isn't met, at least we are able to understand what has happened and can both honor our effort and lament our falling short.

We Can Easily Determine Which Ministries Are Essential

What is the church? What does a congregation require to be a church? What can we cut and still be ourselves? We see some aspects of church life as optional or expendable, and others as core or essential. When the going gets tough, programs and ministries we see as expendable are cut. But we need to discern very carefully and prayerfully what belongs in which category, whether the optional things are truly optional and whether the core things are as unavoidable and unchangeable as they may seem.

Neoliberal capitalism and other mainstream ways of thinking assume any organization's goals are growth and survival ("more is better!"). They lead us to prioritize the things that are most likely to lead to these goals and cut the things that don't. Some books about Christian steward-ship offer concrete recommendations for congregational priorities. They tend to place outreach, social justice, and service to community members who aren't strong financial givers (for example, youth) on an optional list. From what we know about Jesus, though, these are the very ministries he would prioritize. I know discernment about church min-istries isn't as simple as saying "let's prioritize what Jesus would prioritize." But that should be a central part of the conversation. Also, who is part of decision-making about priorities matters. What if we committed to the radical work of making truly collective decisions about our money that reflected our core priorities more than our desire to survive or grow?

Moral Proximity Is a Sufficient Guide

Moral proximity is a concept that asserts we are most obligated to help those who are "closest" to us. "The closer the moral proximity of the poor the greater the moral obligation to help… Moral proximity refers to how connected we are to someone by virtue of familiarity, kinship, space, or time."[4] The old chestnut "Think globally, act locally" suggests we are responsible only for people, places, and things that are close at hand. Of course, what we feel responsible for and what we are actually responsible for may differ significantly. When I lead workshops about church finance, people often respond to my call for just financial practices by saying, "Yes, we should do what we can to address inequality within our churches and local communities, but we can't be all things to all people." In other words, we aren't fundamentally responsible for others—and certainly not for everyone and everything.

My question for us all, however, is this: Who are we responsible to and for? The answer is far from simple. On one hand, trying to take responsibility for others can be paternalistic. On the other, saying I am responsible only for myself is contrary to the second Great Commandment: "Love your neighbor as yourself." Even in a globalized and deeply interconnected world, we might never see or know the people or parts of the planet our actions could severely impact. Although we generally feel closer ties to the people we know personally—and even greater ties to those we like—core tenets of the Christian tradition disrupt the notion that that is who we are accountable to.

In both Matthew's and Luke's Gospels, we see Jesus disrupting familial relationships and instructing his followers to prioritize those who are more "distant." Regarding disruption, we hear "they will be divided: father against son, and son against father, mother against daughter and daughter against mother" (Luke 12:53, Matthew 10:35). Continuing in the tradition of the Hebrew scriptures, he commands us to care for the alien, the stranger, and the foreigner. Jesus challenges our usual relationship hierarchies, saying, for example, "You have heard that it was said, 'You shall love your neighbor and hate your enemy.' But I say to you, love your enemy and pray for those who persecute you" (Matthew 5:43–44).

Conventional notions of moral proximity can make a lot of practical sense, and I am not advocating we toss them all out. If you trip and fall right next to me, I should reach out my hand and help you get back up. If you fall on the other side of town or on the other side of the world, whoever is close by should be the one to help you. I don't need to jump on a plane to help you up. If everyone helps those close to them, everyone who needs it will get helped. Right? But that is far too simple a metaphor for our complex world. Most situations of harm are much more complicated than someone tripping and require "help" that is also more complex and that we aren't all able to offer. I do not believe it is possible for us to act as though we are equally responsible to every person and creature on Earth. I do believe, however, that Jesus challenges us to subvert conventional lines of moral accountability, prioritize those on the margins, and recognize our complicity and capability in diverse and complex situations of harm and injustice—particularly if we possess social, economic, and racial dominance and privilege. Systems of inequality and injustice in our world are such that those who are physically or emotionally "closer" to us are likely to share the level of privilege or marginalization we have. Therefore, those with greater capacity to give are likely to be more connected to each other than to those in greater need. Those who are marginalized often lack connections to those whose privilege and power could really make a difference. If we think of ourselves as primarily morally accountable to those we know, those who are relatively privileged or marginalized will remain so. We need to reach across divides and strive to care just as much about the suffering of a stranger as we would if it were our own.

These dynamics apply not only to individuals but to congregations and other communities. In a relatively wealthy church in the Global North, members may have access to various forms of wealth, power, and influence. Many will have disposable funds available for various causes, space in their homes that could be shared with others, and time to volunteer and care for those in need. For example, I have been part of churches where listservs and bulletin boards offer affordable or free rooms in members' homes (in exchange for light housekeeping and companionship for an elder, for example), free tickets for musical or sporting events that would otherwise go unused, free assistance with childcare, or tutoring by seniors eager to connect with different generations and be of service. These offers can help to build a sense of community and a shared network of support, and when my own finances were tighter, I was deeply grateful for the opportunities they presented. Yet when many in the congregation enjoy similar levels of privilege, the possibilities for radical redistribution are less than they could be if there were more diversity. Studies about taxation and funding arrangements (for example, using more localized or larger tax bases to fund public schools) show us how local funding models further inequality (as this leads to wealthier people funding only the schools in their own, already privileged, neighborhoods), whereas more centralized models focus additional resources wherever there is most need and transfer resources from wealthier to poorer areas. These findings might be applicable to church contexts as well. Which funding arrangement sounds more like what Jesus would do?

Do You Recognize These Idols?

Do you recognize any of these idols, values that often undergird church finance? Have you encountered them in your own life or in situations in your church community? Did seeing them here make you feel defensive, uncomfortable, or maybe vindicated, like you knew something wasn't right but weren't sure how to name it? I know when I started looking at topics such as church finance and fundraising critically, I felt overwhelmed. I wasn't sure how to begin to do anything differently. I was afraid to approach stewardship in a new way. Feelings can be easily hurt; it's risky for a pastor to mess with the system that pays your bills; and

I might cause tensions with the people I am trying to serve. But I have found more openness among church leaders to these ideas than I initially expected and hope you will too.

At the same time, fear is a very real emotion and important to address. Many people have fears related to their own financial security. Many fear offending others if they try to talk about privilege or specific practices related to money. Talking about money can be awkward. Many people are afraid their church will close and a community that has been very important to them won't be able to serve them or the next generation. That fear is increased when people think their leadership and decisions might determine whether a church community survives. While these fears are valid, talking about them openly with one another and with God can be liberating, and we can create a sense of deep community and solidarity in doing so.

Fundraising and budgeting can be tough to do critically and faithfully. So often we dance around these topics or approach them again and again in the same old ways. We might base this year's budget largely on last year's, raise funds each year for the same organizations with the same events, or pray generally, week after week, for "the poor." But I do think many congregations are interested in asking big-picture questions related to our personal resources, those of our church community, and justice, such as why poverty exists and what can be done not merely to alleviate but eradicate it.

Many church members hunger for discussions about money that are more open and honest. Some people who are wealthy and privileged and also aware of their status in the world feel uncomfortable about what they have, how they got it, and what they should do about it. People who are marginalized and lack resources are often heartened to learn that the challenges they face are tied to broader systems, and they are eager to discuss how change could be possible for themselves and others. Conversations about money—whether personal, communal, or systemic—are usually challenging. But when we begin to engage deeper questions, seeking our truest vocation and dreaming of approaches to money that are progressive and faithful, possibilities begin to emerge for us. Many fundraisers and financial leaders I have known are tired of conventional thank-you letters and stewardship campaigns. Many pastors are bored with preaching again and again on the same passages in "stewardship season." We may be tired, uncertain, or afraid. But I do believe that when we go forth in bold compassion, are honest about our own complicity and shortcomings, and invite others into a compelling vision for justice in and through community practices, we can find great cause for hope. In the next chapter, with our eyes open to some of the assumptions we've uncovered here, I'll show you how we can begin to approach church finance in new ways.

3.

Through a Lens of Justice
Reimagining Church Practices

I hope you have noticed the distance between the sources of our moral and ethical deliberation that we examined in chapter 1 and the stories we found that our financial practices are telling in chapter 2. We have seen that our financial frameworks are rooted in a different system of meaning, drawing on values that are different from, and in some cases are opposed to, our most cherished notions of justice and faith. The guiding frameworks we use to make financial decisions might prevent us from living into our commitments to justice, or they may ignite a powerful witness to these commitments. Our operating values affect how we approach features of church life such as land ownership and location; buildings; investments; staffing and volunteer leadership; relationship to other churches and communities; and nonprofit status. I know this is a lot to think about, but just because we don't know if we can do this work of alignment perfectly doesn't mean we shouldn't start somewhere. We need to continually reconsider these aspects of our church life —a justice analysis won't simply be something we can undertake once and consider it "done." But every step we take toward bringing our core values to bear on our financial practices brings us closer to realizing God's vision of an equitable and just world for all creation.

This work might be new or challenging to some people. Often the people who are most excited about working for justice are not involved in the administration or management of church life. Many think of a "steward" as one who preserves assets for the next generation, and those who serve in these areas may feel comfortable with conventional financial and fundraising practices and think doing things in new ways is too risky or not really necessary. The perceived risk can be magnified by a sense of responsibility to the past and desire that the church exist long into the future. Or leaders may feel tired, busy, and over-committed, perhaps under-appreciated—because much of their work goes on behind the scenes—and therefore resistant to considering yet one more complex task. My best advice is to acknowledge these concerns directly and also to reframe notions like responsibility and stewardship as matters of faithfulness to God and the gospel, rather than to particular traditions, procedures, or physical structures. The goal is to pass on to future generations not property but an exciting, vibrant, countercultural manifestation of God's love. Those who are tired and overwhelmed might also be invited to think about how this reimagining might simplify church life, especially aspects that require a great deal of time and money.

Some of us who are involved in the financial aspect of church work are thinking about legacy—our own and that of the institutions we have supported—as we age. We might be culling through possessions, differentiating between tangible assets and the true gifts and values that really matter to us, and asking what efforts we want to support through planned giving or bequests. That mindset can be helpful to this work as well. These issues can be raised in settings like worship, retreats, or vulnerable small group or one-on-one pastoral conversations. The conversations aren't always easy. Fruitful conversations begin with relationships, which depend on our knowing one another's stories, values, commitments, worries, and so forth. If we can help one another to see how we can bring about justice by aligning our finances with who we are and what we value—individually and collectively—this work can be meaningful and even transformative for all involved.

Land and Location

A first step in our quest for justice-rooted church finance is to consider the place where your community is located. The history of your particular place can be difficult and complex—spiritually and practically. The traumatic history of European colonization throughout the world involves Indigenous lands being stolen and Indigenous peoples being displaced. It is critical to ask questions about how your church came to be where it is, what traditional Indigenous territory you are benefitting from, and how you are participating in the occupation of it (unless your congregation is itself Indigenous). Many excellent resources are available online, including Native Land Digital, that can show the Indigenous communities, languages, and treaties that are related to your community's location. Indigenous peoples have not only a long and vibrant history but are also living communities. The people on whose traditional territory your church is located might now live elsewhere, and other Indigenous peoples and communities might have taken their place. Getting to know the specific history of the land where you are is an important exercise unto itself, in order to better understand how colonization took place and to recognize and honor the traditional stewards of the land. It should also lead us to develop relationships with contemporary Indigenous communities and organizations. Although your church may have come into being long after the process of colonization began, you still benefit from the land and space, and the traditional inhabitants of the territory are still impacted.

It is also important to consider the history of your congregation and its neighborhood with respect to other racial and class legacies and dynamics. Who has lived in the community where you are located throughout the decades? How has your congregation related to its neighbors in various time periods? In some cases, predominantly white churches moved from city neighborhoods to suburbs, participating in "white flight," furthering the economic downturn of urban areas, and contributing to the loss of affordable community meeting spaces and community services. Is your church located in an "up-and-coming" neighborhood that is experiencing gentrification, contributing to population displacement and racial shift, and displacing existing community networks, businesses, and possibly even churches?

Ethicist Joe Pettit describes how predominantly white churches and denominations have participated in "housing apartheid," implicitly and explicitly supporting and anchoring whites-only communities in suburban areas. By opening churches in racially restrictive communities, churches endorsed racial discrimination and the many resulting oppressions. Conversely, he argues that if these churches had refused to open in whites-only suburbs, this racist practice likely would have ended.[1] Because of the high moral standing of these denominations in society at the time, their boycott of these suburbs would have been powerful. For these reasons and others, both the presence and absence of privileged churches in a community can have a significant impact, so it is important to examine local history through a race- and class-informed lens.

The ecology and watershed of the land where your church is situated also has implications for just stewardship practices. The work of activist theologian Ched Meyers related to watershed discipleship offers a helpful theological perspective.[2] It is important to investigate the ecological web where your church is located and to understand how to be well integrated into that ecosystem as one species among many. It is also important to learn how climate change is impacting and will impact your community. We need to learn how to live sustainably and respectfully where we are—what sort of landscaping and building practices (including retrofits) are best suited to the local ecology to minimize negative environmental impacts and maximize environmental benefits. Some of these changes may be complicated, but the climate crisis makes the need to change our practices increasingly critical. Seeking deep understanding of your location is one step toward "greening" your church and reducing your environmental/carbon footprints, regardless of where you are located.

Once we know more about our history and the place where we are located, what do we do? We can make amends for broken relationships and strive to live into right relationships going forward. One way to live into right relationships with Indigenous communities is to contribute to a reparations-based land tax. Where I live, on Ohlone land in what is colonially known as Northern California, Shuumi Land Tax (*shuumi* means gift in the Chochenyo language) provides a way for non-Indigenous people to acknowledge the land where they are located by contributing to a fund called the Sogorea Te' Land Trust.[3] This organization works to return Indigenous land to Indigenous communities, so they can restore traditional practices—for example, by establishing a cemetery for Ohlone ancestral remains and creating ceremonial spaces. Individuals, businesses, churches, and other organizations can participate in this project through offerings of time, advocacy, and financial gifts. Similar initiatives exist in other places. Where formal land tax programs don't yet exist, developing relationships with local Indigenous communities and inquiring about appropriate reparations can lead to contextually appropriate ways to honor the land and its peoples.

Another powerful witness to justice, the #LandBack movement, encourages non-Indigenous people, including churches, to demonstrate their commitment to reconciliation by returning land to Indigenous communities. For example, an undeveloped piece of land purchased by the United Church of Canada in Southern Ontario in the 1960s was returned to an Indigenous organization in 2017.[4] The Rocky Mountain Synod of the Evangelical Lutheran Church in America transferred the deed for property in the city of Denver that had already been a site for Indigenous community programs for decades. Many other examples of engagement, ranging from payment of land taxes to entire land transfers, exist. Related conversations could be had with other groups and communities, such as those displaced by gentrification, housing discrimination, Japanese concentration (commonly referred to as internment) camps, and many other oppressive practices. While some of us may take our place for granted, simply existing where we are is not a neutral act. Although we can't undo every past harm, we can strive to develop relationships, make reparations, and support work for justice today.

Property and Physical Structures

Buildings can be a revenue generator *and* they can also be a source of great financial drain. They can contribute to climate change, and they can contribute to robust civic and social life in communities. They are not essential, however. Even the old finger rhyme teaches children that the church is not the steepled building but rather the people. Some churches choose not to have buildings—while others cannot afford them. In some denominations, the buildings are owned not by the congregation but instead by denominational bodies, so congregations may have less of a say in these decisions.

Communities that are able to choose whether to own a building, rent space, or have a physical meeting place at all can generally list valid reasons to go in any of these directions. Money spent maintaining a large physical structure that is owned by a church is tied up and not available for other efforts, but many churches use their buildings for significant community service and appreciate the stability and possibilities for mission they present. Community groups often rely on churches for free or low-cost meeting space. Some churches choose rental arrangements because they are more flexible and can be more affordable. In some cases, these church communities value the collaborative possibilities rental spaces present and appreciate that the rent the church pays will support the owning organization (i.e., school, community center, other religious community, and the like). Churches are thinking creatively about space in a whole variety of ways. For example, some churches are exploring the possibility of transferring their property to a community organization that would maintain the structure and manage rental groups, one of which might be the church. A church might downsize and divest itself of some portion of its property or share space with another organization or faith community. Outdoor possibilities, such as forest churches or gathering in parks, can work very well in some locations and for some communities and can further an environment-focused mission.

Other possibilities exist on the spectrum between owning a great deal of property and structures and having none. The movement toward house churches, small groups that meet for worship in people's homes, has emerged, faded, and reemerged over time. This model has many benefits, including the intimacy of the gatherings and the (much!) lower operating costs. On the other hand, people generally need to be invited to participate in such groups, making it difficult for possible new members and visitors to find their way in. People with urgent needs, including those who are unhoused, are also unlikely to be able to find support in house churches, while many churches with physical structures can offer a place of welcome, safety, and even referrals to social services. Communities without buildings often end up being demographically homogeneous because people invite others they know, people like them. A church building is at least semi-public and visible to the community. Church signs offer public witness, sharing messages with the broader community as people pass by. Church buildings can offer sanctuary to refugees facing deportation and spaces for people to gather in natural disasters and other emergencies. As visible symbols of Christianity, they are accessible for public critique and even protest. That may seem strange to note, but because the church has participated in many atrocities, faith communities with an identifiable church building can rightfully receive those grievances and accept responsibility for what has happened. This symbolic role is not possible if faith communities are scattered among people's homes or in rented spaces in buildings primarily used for other purposes and that don't "look like" churches. I'm not arguing that these limitations justify having a building. Creative solutions to some of the downsides of house churches or rental spaces, such as including well-designed signage and a vibrant online presence, can be developed. The COVID-19 pandemic has demonstrated that worship and other aspects of church life do not require physical structures. Rather than claiming buildings are necessary or always an impediment, we can carefully think through their role, guided by our commitments to justice and our contextual realities, priorities, and needs.

Investments

The Bible doesn't say much about investing in the way we think about it now, but it has a lot to say about usury—an old-fashioned term that means charging an excessive amount of interest to a person who has fallen on hard times and needs a loan. For some people, such as farmers who could only sell their crops once a year, "hard times" were not exceptional but quite common and predictable. In ancient times, there were no rules about how much interest you could charge, and so ordinary people were at the mercy of local lenders' greed and on the hook for enormous sums out of proportion to what they borrowed out of necessity. Not surprisingly, then, many religions restrict these lending practices.

When we think about usury today, the situation at first seems quite different. While exploitative lending certainly takes place in our society, we might think that neither we as individuals nor our churches collectively are lending money exploitatively, so usury rules wouldn't apply. But usury fundamentally is about people with money using it to make more money off the backs of people with less money. It's about the rich getting richer while the poor go deeper into debt. And it's about thinking "what's mine is mine," so I might as well put it to work for me.

Churches do not typically make loans, or if they do, the terms aren't generally exploitative. But investing is about using our money to make more money. By its very nature, investing is restricted to people, churches, and entities that have more money than they need in the moment. People who are barely making ends meet do not invest. Investing widens the gap between the rich and the poor. Choosing to invest money implies that our future needs (and wants) take precedence over someone else's present needs. Because in our society, we do not have a robust system to care for one another's needs, investing and saving for the future is a completely reasonable response to the way our society is structured. But we need to recognize the choice we are making. When we as churches and as individuals put money away or invest it, we should hear John the Baptist speaking into our ear, "'Whoever has two coats must share with anyone who has none; and whoever has food must do likewise" (Luke 3:11).

Churches already recognize that investing can be morally complicated. Many churches have rules against investing in so-called sin industries, such as pornography or tobacco. Some churches and denominations have made rules against investing in companies that finance or contribute to the climate crisis. In an attempt to make our investing more ethical, we might try to invest only in industries with just labor standards and environmental practices. We might even try to invest in ways that seek to do good rather than harm, lifting up companies that create positive social impact or investing in BIPOC (Black, Indigenous, and people of color)-owned businesses. Ethical investing is getting easier; we can even choose money managers who will follow our specific criteria.

But questions about whether to invest our money are still based on the assumption that it is rightfully ours. Like everything in our churches, money has its own origin story. Who or what has been impacted along the path the money has traveled on its way to us? Some churches have money that was earned through the labor of enslaved people. Others have money that was given by generations of white people who were not hindered in their wealth building by red-lining and who benefitted from racist housing policies.

I know there is a lot to think about, but I don't want us to be immobilized by these questions. No one's money is ethically "pure." But when we make decisions about money, we should see it for what it is and where it has come from.

Even churches that don't have, for example, direct historical ties to slavery might still need to ask questions about their money. I know of a church that had a budget surplus and money available to invest because they charged high rent to the organizations that used their building. Because space was limited in the community, groups were willing to pay, but church leaders could have asked whether this "excess" was a sign that the rental fees should be reconsidered, particularly in light of the marginalized communities many of the groups served (groups the church often celebrated as part of their own community service).

Often, churches invest as a way to ensure we will have funds in the future, determining that having money in the future outweighs the possible uses for that money now. We might invest our capital to produce ongoing income, which we can use to fund our work and deal with the uncertainty that the future offers. We might strive to do so in a way that has the most positive impact, selecting companies and funds committed to social and ecological good (known as impact investing) and avoiding those that cause harm (divestment). The size of our investments might not make these decisions matter on a grand scale, but when we participate alongside others, such as in a large-scale divestment campaign, our collective impact adds up. We might also choose to remain as shareholders in companies that participate in injustice, so we have the right to attend shareholder meetings and demand companies make changes (known as shareholder advocacy). Of course, that work takes a great deal of time and expertise, but it can be done and can have an impact.

Ethical or socially responsible investing is a common approach in churches. A lot of banks and credit unions have funds that are already set up to make this relatively easy to do. These funds may positively select for companies that support principles such as environmental steward-ship, human rights, and racial/gender justice. Or they may primarily screen out companies with negative social impacts, such as those engaged with alcohol, firearms and weapons, tobacco, gambling, and fossil fuels. Selecting such funds can be complicated, because some companies do a variety of things. For example, some fossil fuel companies are now getting involved with renewable energy. But this sort of investing, while imperfect, enables us to live into our values, in part, through our investments.

A minister I know works for a large, wealthy church with substantial endowments—totaling over $25 million. She told me many of her church members are afraid to use any of these funds—or even discuss the possibility of it—because of their sense that their primary obligation is to ensure that their congregation will exist as long as possible into the future. In our conversation, she shared some of her complex thoughts about these funds, even though they are invested in explicitly ethical portfolios. She noted that church members do not question where the money that is invested came from in the first place. Sources include wealth that originated in slavery, and more recently donations made by people working in exploitative industries. She wonders if it is right to continue to use the proceeds from these funds and what reparations might be made to those who have been impacted by their creation. For the time being, the church offers grants to other churches and organizations that do good, but this strategy still allows them to maintain control of who receives how much. She is now working with a small group from the church to eventually hand over control of the investments, to give communities who were directly and indirectly impacted by the monies that were invested the authority to decide how those funds should be used.

In addition, this church is considering living into its values by sharing their fundraising staff position with another community organization. They realize the ability to raise funds is itself a privilege that further entrenches that privilege, as not all churches and communities have someone with the time and expertise to raise and manage funds and fundraising projects. Churches and organizations that have funds to invest can pay some of their bills or fund special projects through investment income and even use some of that money to hire fundraisers to increase the size of the endowment—and therefore their earnings. Those churches that don't have funds to invest must constantly raise money from within their community, where money is generally tighter to begin with. Because investing is more complicated than it seems, we should take the injunction against usury to heart as we think about who's paying the price when our investments are making money for us.

Staffing and Volunteer Leadership

Congregations in most mainline denominations have both paid staff and volunteer leaders. Determining what is done by staff and what is done by volunteers is itself an ethical deliberation. Further, even the framework of "volunteering" is complex. For some, the term suggests that it is optional and represents going above and beyond what is required as a church member and as a follower of Jesus, whereas others think contributing our time and skills (in addition to our financial resources) is an obligation. Some think classifying a role as volunteer leads people to take it less seriously and argue that we should think of all people serving the church—paid or unpaid—as ministers. Although I believe that is a meaningful argument, I use the term "volunteer" to describe work that is unpaid. But the decision about whether to pay someone for their work is freighted.

Much work in churches is done by volunteers. What volunteering versus being paid means varies in different contexts and for different people. In one church where I served in ministry, people commented to me that they were saddened to hear we were going to be hiring paid children's ministry leaders. To them, it was a sign that no one wanted to do this work and that paying people was the only way we could convince someone to do it. Some were sad that we were "outsourcing" our children's ministry to people who might not have any particular connection to our church and who might see the work as "just a job." To others, though, paying these leaders was an exciting sign that the church was finally willing to compensate people (mostly women) for this work and show that we valued children's ministry. Paying people ensured we had skilled, consistent, accountable leaders rather than constantly changing rosters of whoever was willing to be guilted into taking on the job that week. Some people saw paying workers as the church finally getting with the times and recognizing that women, who had done this work for decades, were now largely employed and should not be expected to teach for free on top of everything else they were doing. Some questioned why having paid children's staff was noteworthy, while having a paid minister, music director, or custodian was not.

For people with stable and adequate incomes, volunteering can be a wonderful addition to one's life. For those without financial security, paid employment can be life-changing for oneself, one's family, and generations to come. From a justice perspective, however, compensating people adequately for their work is generally understood as important. However, for some volunteers, the opportunity to serve can help them to feel like they are part of something larger than themselves and are making a contribution to the church and community, even if they lack the means to do so financially. It can give people important experience, skills, and a sense of purpose and belonging. It can also give people access to opportunities that they might not be otherwise qualify for, offering them experiences that will help them with future employment. Retirees with adequate financial resources, for example, often appreciate the opportunity to offer their skills and expertise and the sense of structure and community volunteering provides.

The decision about whether to pay someone for a given task is often based on whether it is possible to get someone to do it as a volunteer, whether a church can afford to pay for the work, and the culture of the church community about which roles have historically been paid or not. Congregations can reach different but still ethical conclusions about whether to use volunteers or paid staff, but it is important to ask questions other than simply, "How can we get the most work for the least amount of money?" For example, we might ask who in our church or community is excluded from or facing barriers to employment and consider what role the church might play. I've known churches that have created small paid jobs for people who have fallen on hard times, even though someone else might have done the work for free or the work might not even have been absolutely necessary to begin with. I knew a church that created paid roles (assisting with meals and refreshments) for people with intellectual disabilities who initially faced employment barriers but, because of their experience working at church, were able to go on to other forms of paid employment. Sometimes, churches have worked with others to create good, full-time, paid, shared staffing positions that they couldn't afford on their own. I've also known churches that, after much discernment, have decided to simplify their structure, hire incredibly minimal paid staff, rely extensively on volunteers, and primarily allocate their budget for community advocacy work. Other churches decide to simply shrink their budgets, so members can devote their money to the causes that are most important to them.

The philosophy of "most work for least pay" is often seen in how jobs are structured in church contexts. Because some church-related tasks are flexible, variable, and behind-the-scenes, churches might not understand those tasks as labor worthy of compensation. But paid workers are not always treated justly. Under neoliberal economic systems, work is increasingly precarious—part-time, seasonal, outsourced, highly variable, and easily terminated. Some churches participate in this system. For example, as their needs vary throughout the year (for example, with higher attendance in certain seasons), they hire employees for only the parts of the year with higher attendance, putting their employment on hold during the summer or other lower-need seasons. They follow this practice even though a worker's expenses do not cease in the summer months, and this can be a great time to complete less urgent tasks or take compensatory time off for excess hours worked during the program year. A culture of easy dismissal generally means workers are more likely to do what their employers or others with greater power in the system want—even if the work is unsafe.

To save money, churches might shift work that had been done by an employee (for example, janitorial services) to an outside company, which often means the church no longer knows how much the staff are paid or what their working arrangements are. Using outside companies might be the right answer in some cases, but just practices require that we ask why they are being considered and what the ramifications are for the workers. Some businesses we contract may have excellent labor practices and even be social enterprises, helping people find employment who might otherwise face barriers (for example, due to disability, status as formerly incarcerated people, and so forth). Regardless, it is our responsibility to try to ensure that everyone is paid adequately and has good working conditions as we strive to pursue justice through our practices.

The most important question to consider is, What values are guiding our decisions? When we step back and look at who and how much we pay for what, do we see justice practiced? Are we paying people in certain roles more because they genuinely have greater responsibilities and require greater training and skills, or does that choice simply reflect what is commonplace and biases regarding gender, race, or other factors? Does the labor market set our wage scale, or do we think about other factors, such as what constitutes a living wage where we are located? Are we sure that workers have received the training they need, have adequate support, receive appropriate and respectful supervision, have safe working conditions, and so on? If work is being done by volunteers, are we sure this is a fulfilling arrangement for them? Are there people in our community who need more work than they have? Of course, churches cannot simply employ every person in need, but on a small scale we can model the just practices we desire for everyone. At the same time, we need to advocate for just policies that will impact us all, such as a strong social safety net, so losing one's job is not a matter of life or death. Churches, as employers and as recipients of volunteer labor, can and should model their values as much as possible in their cultures, policies, and practices of work.

Relationship to Other Churches and Communities

Mainline Protestant congregations tend to promote the ways they are different from other faith communities, which focus primarily on their own congregations, rather than a denomination and Christianity generally. The extent of this separation varies between traditions and denominations. Some congregations are connected to others, whether formally or informally, and others are explicitly independent. Even in congregations whose members have warm feelings toward the wider church, when it comes to church finance, we generally operate largely on our own. If we can't make our budget, we need to cut. If we still can't make it work, we close. Conversely, if we have endowments, we might assume we can exist indefinitely, regardless of whether we are having any impact in the community or have any members in our pews. Some denominations do have funds to help struggling churches or grants for certain types of ministries, but such support generally is relatively minimal. Sometimes churches struggle financially because demographics are changing—people are moving out of the community, or it is becoming more religiously diverse—and maintaining a congregation might not make sense. Other times a church has simply reached the end of its life cycle for other reasons. But when we let money (and privilege) rather than mission or meaning dictate which churches stay open and which do not, we do a disservice to our values. Some churches can stay open indefinitely due to their endowments, rental income, or even just one very large giver. And others that are offering vital ministries to marginalized communities might still close because the model that each church funds itself doesn't work for them. When we take a step back and look at the big picture, we see that often the inequalities of our world (based on race, class, immigration status, gender, sexuality, and so forth) are also characteristics of churches that are more likely to just scrape by and face closure.

Most churches that are part of denominations do share their wealth, to some extent, by giving to their denomination. However, leaders and members often treat these contributions as something they have to pay but don't benefit much from. They wonder whether the contribution is "worth it," whether some churches are "free-riding" because of these funds, or denominational executives are sitting around in fancy offices doing little. Feelings about giving to the wider church often mirror people's feelings about taxes and government, with some thinking sharing funds is an unnecessary burden and others thinking it's a strategy for rectifying inequalities and supporting those going through hardship. Some people recognize that denominations, like governments, can provide important services that are hard for congregations to support on their own and are best done collectively. Just as we want government workers to show up when there's a natural disaster, we want to know a denominational lawyer will respond to our phone call after we learn our church is being sued. And just as more privileged people often think they don't need government support because they can just pay directly for what they need and want, larger churches often do need to rely less on their denominations. But that doesn't mean that they shouldn't contribute for those who do need those services, such as worship resources, legal advice, specialized ministries, political advocacy work, and so forth.

On a smaller scale, churches often collaborate with those that are geographically closest to them, especially in the same denomination. They may share programming, occasional worship, even some staff, and so forth. Sometimes on this local level, we can really feel and see the inequality and divides that separate our churches. Going into one another's spaces, we can experience the differing sizes, levels of upkeep, and so forth. We may know and even discuss the reasons behind these differences, but we may not know what to do about them. For example, when multiple churches share staff, it may feel easiest for each church to pay an equal share (or a share based on size), pretending that various forms of inequality don't exist or not wanting to shame poorer churches that may well take pride in their contribution. But as we know with individuals, paying the same amount doesn't require the same level of sacrifice. To address inequality, we have to be able to talk about how it has arisen and how it is experienced. At times it is right for one church to give more or do more— depending on ability and need. These insights from local collaborations can be a stepping-stone that helps church leaders and members see beyond their local contexts, to look at bigger missional questions instead of the "what will benefit me most?" standard. We need to think of other churches not as competition but as siblings in the one body of Christ and our contributions to the wider church not as an encumbrance but as a way to be church together, to speak prophetically in a united voice, to bear one another's burdens, and to make reparations to those who have been harmed.

Nonprofit Status and the Nonprofit Industrial Complex

Part of the structure of church life for most churches in North America is that they operate both officially and

culturally as nonprofit organizations. The legal requirements and benefits of nonprofit status vary, and in some
cases churches can choose whether to register as nonprofits. When churches have a choice, they might ask
whether the benefits outweigh the costs—and yes, there
are costs. For example, I worked for a nonprofit organization that grappled with the limitations on nonprofits'
political advocacy work as we discerned whether the tax
benefits to donors outweighed these limitations and considered whether people would still donate at the same level
without these tax benefits. Another church had to limit its
advocacy-related expenses because of legal restrictions
when they embarked on a significant lobbying campaign
related to passing Indigenous justice legislation. This
campaign was ultimately successful, and because of their
efforts many other churches became engaged in Indigenous solidarity endeavors. However, the project faced an
internal challenge: some people in that community thought
the legal restrictions on nonprofits were too cumbersome
and they should forgo their status, and others believed any
political advocacy work was not appropriate because of
their nonprofit status (despite the fact that laws limit but do
not completely restrict this work).

Speaking broadly, activists and scholars are exploring
the way the structure of nonprofit entities can actually
preserve and perpetuate systemic inequality, even if they
were founded for the opposite purpose. When they talk about
this problem, they call it the Nonprofit Industrial Complex
(NPIC), a concept introduced in *The Revolution Will Not
Be Funded: Beyond the Non-Profit Industrial Complex* by
the collective INCITE! Women of Color Against Violence.

One of the contributors, Ana Clarissa Rojas Durazo, writes about the development of nonprofits that address violence against women. She describes the early organizing, which was community-based and involved women who had experienced violence and who supported one another.[5] Over time, however, she argues that carrying out this work through professional nonprofits with external funders has influenced and changed the work. For example, the work became professionalized and de-politicized and engaged more in therapeutic services rather than mutual empowerment and social transformation. This shift changed our understanding of the very notion of violence against women. Rather than being treated by society as a systemic social justice issue, violence against women is an issue that has become individualized and pathologized, seen as a "behavioral, criminal, and medical phenomenon."[6] If we see violence against women as a societal justice issue, we need to take collective action. But if we see it as a series of singular tragedies happening to individual women, it is much easier to offer treatment and support to individuals after the fact. There is no motivation to examine factors such as policy and culture.

A major aspect of NPIC critique is that rather than seeking social transformation, "nonprofitization" encourages organizations to accept social injustice as largely inevitable and to address its impacts rather than its root causes—by engaging in political advocacy, for example. Political advocacy work might be prohibited by law for nonprofits beyond a certain amount, but nonprofits might also be more subtly impacted by funders' agendas. Also, by alleviating the situation just enough to make it tolerable (at least for some people), the work of nonprofits can serve to quell the urge towards more radical change.

Although churches are not the same as social service–related nonprofits, many do engage in some social-justice advocacy, either directly or indirectly. Depending on what version of history we look at, we can see ways the church has been serving people's basic needs for centuries—and pushing society and government to protect human rights and care for all people. Both are part of the history, but which one we emphasize matters. Those who want to cut government spending are more than happy to have churches and nonprofits pick up the slack and serve those basic needs, and we need to be aware of that. Are we so busy trying to help with survival needs that we don't have time—or think it our place—to ask why these needs aren't being met in the first place? Are we biting our tongues and reshaping our work to maintain our nonprofit status and thereby allowing government entities (keeping in mind that in democracies, governments are "us") and corporations off the hook for big-picture change? Does operating within the nonprofit framework limit our imaginations as well as our legal capabilities to work for justice? In these conversations, I often think of the quote from liberation theologian and Catholic archbishop Hélder Pessoa Câmara: "When I give food to the poor they call me a saint. When I ask why they are poor they call me a communist."[7] I am not suggesting we shouldn't assist people who are suffering, but we also need to ask how we can prevent suffering from occurring in the first place. Does being a nonprofit help or hinder us in that work? It probably depends, but I think it is good to keep in mind that nonprofit status is not a pure and uncriticized good and that some who have studied this issue worry that nonprofit status can steer communities away from more fundamental questions about and work for systemic change.

Living Out Our Convictions

These are just a few aspects of church financial life that can be considered through a lens of justice. I hope you are starting to see some consistent principles and values—that privilege and oppression lead to financial divides and that we need to critically consider history, share resources across divides, bring churches and people together to work collaboratively, and embody our ethics in how we approach financial decisions and priorities. I hope you are beginning to see ways that the values of faith and the values of money are in conflict in church life. In the next chapter, I will speak more explicitly about a vision for justice-rooted church finance.

In the meantime, I hear you thinking: but wait! As a congregation we are just barely making ends meet as it is! How can we do these things that feel risky and countercultural and that might negatively impact our financial situation even more? To that I say, yes, I hear your concerns. But what better way to practice living our faith in ways that really matter—and that really witness to our convictions? Churches on the underside of privilege have known these risks and realities for far too long. And at the same time, I believe we need to share risk better, so we can truly be church for one and all, rather than leaving some members of the body to struggle alone. If we had safety nets within our churches that allowed individuals to share more extravagantly, knowing there would be help and support no matter what the outcome of their magnanimous giving, what could we accomplish? What if these safety nets also existed between churches, so any given congregation could know that others would step in to help if they took a risk in the name of justice that left them in a bind?

4.

The Foolish Way of Jesus

Practicing Christian Community

By now I hope you are feeling at least curious about how you and your congregation might bring your practices into better alignment with what you believe. If you feel convinced that church financial practices are important to reconsider, you may be wondering what comes next. Church finance is deeply integrated into who and what the church is. So, we can't change what we do with our money without thinking about the church as a whole—what we think the church is for and what it could and should be. We also need to reflect on our commitments and our practices, making sure that they are in alignment. I like to use the model of a hermeneutic spiral where action and reflection are understood as an ongoing process, each leading back into the other. We won't always get it "right," and what is "right" is constantly evolving. We begin, though, by reflecting on what the church is and what it is for.

What Is the Church?

Some people think of the church as primarily a human-created institution, and others see it as created or shaped primarily by God. This dichotomy is an oversimplification, of course. Most of us probably land somewhere in the middle of that spectrum. Each perspective both offers wisdom and presents potential pitfalls for engaging justice issues. Those who see the church in its present form as directly instituted by God might think critique and change are contrary to God's intent. On the other hand, they might see change, especially change toward justice, as required of us in order to restore or achieve God's intent for the church. Those who see the church as primarily a human creation might view changes and critiques as necessary steps in the church's ongoing formation. Or they might feel pressure not to make changes, given the weight of tradition and continuity in their hands.

A related issue is the purpose of the church as understood in different traditions. If we think the church is an expression of faith, embodying what we believe, then its form and whether that aligns with God's vision is crucial. If we understand the church to be a "means to an end" (whether that "end" is sharing Christian faith, accomplishing mission, or something else), we might focus on these outcomes and take a utilitarian view of the form of the church itself. Whether we think of the church as instituted by God or created by people, whether we see it as important in itself or as a tool affects the way we approach questions related to justice in church practice. For example, it will help you to know whether to emphasize justice as integral to God's nature or to show how justice can aid in the end your community seeks to achieve. This isn't to be manipulative—I believe both are true—but rather to help you to know where to start.

Understanding how your congregation views the church and its mission helps determine what framework for conversations about justice in church finance will resonate best in your own context. Communities that value tradition will want to see how justice has been embedded in the church since its earliest expressions. They will likely want to know how the thinking of important church leaders and theologians from your tradition, or even your congregation, relates to your situation today. Traditionally, Catholic and Orthodox churches have focused on the church as a divine creation, while Protestant churches have emphasized the idea that the church is a human creation. However, since Vatican II, the Catholic Church has begun to use images of the church as a pilgrim people and the people of God, which focus more on the church as an evolving, contextual community. In some Protestant traditions, the idea that there are two churches—one visible to the world and the other visible to God—underscores that the church as we know it is a human and therefore fallible construct. At the same time, some Protestant traditions de-emphasize the importance of the church to begin with. For example, Anabaptist and Pentecostal traditions have traditionally focused on the relationship between the individual and God, understanding the church as a gathering that primarily supports individual spiritual growth. Communities more focused on outcomes, that see the church as a vehicle for mission, might focus on justice-oriented principles and practices that can strengthen that work. Likely multiple approaches to and understandings of the church are present in any given community, regardless of denominational affiliation and tradition. Many people have had connections with different traditions throughout their lives, and our experiences of particular churches and our own beliefs and journeys impact what we see as important.

One metaphor for the church used by many people who focus on justice is that of *koinonia* or community. Biblical scholar Barbara Rossing writes that this Greek term has been used to encompass relationships that include both friendship and financial partnership.[1] She argues that *koinonia* describes sharing property and the spiritual communion experienced in the Eucharist, and in that way it integrates expressions of material sharing and communal faith.[2] This sharing occurs among not only individuals but churches (of both a spiritual and material nature).[3] In its financial sense, it describes relationships involving obligations from all parties, and as the term came to be used in Christian communities, it retained this practical and embodied meaning.[4]

Rossing believes it is likely from a historical perspective that at least some form of financial sharing across class lines existed in the earliest Christian communities. This practice is confirmed by extra-biblical sources, such as the philosopher Lucian, who was critical of Christian communities for being "gullible," his view of their expressions of generosity.[5] For the early Christians, theological uniformity was not a prerequisite to financial sharing. Rather, it seems even churches that disagreed about issues such as the inclusion of Gentiles participated in this practice.[6] This observation could be relevant to churches and individuals today who use differences of opinion as an excuse to avoid or cease offering financial support to churches (or individuals or organizations) whose beliefs do not align completely with theirs. This is not to suggest that individuals or churches should share resources uncritically, but rather to ask whether the difference of opinion is so serious that money truly cannot be shared in good conscience.

Jürgen Moltmann focuses on the church in his work and has shaped my own understanding. He believes the church is called to anticipate the kingdom of God and to practice on a small scale what we believe God desires for the whole world. This concept has implications for the relationship between work for justice in the world and within the church. Rather than viewing them as competing priorities, we can explore how the two are intertwined. What we experience and create within the church can give us inspiration, hope, and direction for our work in society as well. Theologian Miroslav Volf extends this idea of the church as an anticipation of the kingdom of God, arguing that each congregation is called to be a foretaste of the coming together of all God's people. If we as churches are called to such communion, we must enter into profound relationships with one another and work to rectify any divisions or forms of inequality. But how, practically speaking, do we do that?

Identities, Intersectionality, and Church Finance

Key to our work for justice in the world is our understanding of marginalization and privilege. In general, those who are marginalized because of their identities (as discussed in chapter 1) have less access to resources, capital, influence, and so forth than those who are privileged in most aspects. Not every marginalized aspect of one's identity neatly results in one additional point of economic marginalization.

Identities are intersectional and impact one another, so there's no simple math, but people who hold two or more marginalized identities may experience more than the "sum" of their marginalizations. And of course, even those who appear to be in the same circumstances may not have the same experiences. Since we believe that inequity is unjust and a matter of faith, we need to address it in our churches *and* in society. We need to address the economic impacts of marginalization *and* the very fact that marginalization exists in the first place. We need to explore the ways marginalization and privilege co-create and uphold one another.

Yet, as I described in chapter 2, conventional wisdom says the amount of money and other resources we have is a product of meritocracy. We get what we earn, what we deserve. We even thank God for the resources we have, suggesting that God has decided how much we should have (and how much—or little—others should have too). Although this idea has been de-bunked by many and we might say we don't believe it, we still often operate as though it were true. This harmful ideology ignores the role played by oppressive histories, ongoing systemic causes, and present-day realities that significantly contribute to what and how much we have. It ignores the ways our multiple and intersecting identities consolidate power in some communities and lead to deeply entrenched marginalization in others.

For this reason, even though I wish I could, I am not going to give you a formula for creating just and faithful financial practices in your congregation or in the lives of individuals. We can't approach church finance and fundraising in a one-size-fits-all way, with minor modifications based on how much we have to give. But we can attend to some overarching principles. We must look at church finance within the complex systems of privilege and marginalization that impact us all as individuals and as churches and communities. Examining power and privilege with respect to identity provides a more nuanced perspective on our corporate and personal ethical obligations around finance and fundraising. Doing this also helps us to see how our ethical responsibilities extend far beyond ourselves or our congregation. If we as church leaders take seriously issues of privilege and marginalization, we need to be concerned about all of a person's income and assets (or lack thereof) rather than just the percentage one might give to church. Really contending with inequality may well lead us to initiate social and church transformation that involves the transfer of wealth.

Those who have experienced economic marginalization should be at the center of these conversations and the structures of decision-making, rather than relegating them to the sidelines because they do not have as much wealth to contribute. Theologically, we might recognize God as the force behind the work of redistribution guided by principles of justice, rather than as the source of the status quo of economic inequality or as a mere bystander to all of it. Beginning to reckon with the many ways power and identity intersect might reveal the inadequacy and injustice of conventional approaches to finance and stewardship, as well as offer a guide to live into the values of justice and equality we preach.

How can we do this? We know, for example, that some church financial practices allow economic inequalities to persist, and therefore they (and we) support racial inequality. Acknowledging this, how can our church finance practices further racial justice? One possible response is reparations, which have been called for by Black communities in particular for generations. For example, in 1969, James Foreman, former director of the Student Nonviolent Coordinating Committee, presented the Black Manifesto at the historic Riverside Church in New York City, calling for $500 million in reparations for Black Americans from white churches and synagogues.[7] This echoed earlier calls, such as those made by African Methodist Episcopal Bishop Henry McNeil Turner in the late nineteenth century.[8] Although these calls were not met, and for the most part reparations have not been paid, these calls draw attention to an important component of antiracism work.

In Canada, financial reparations from both the churches that operated Indigenous residential schools and the Canadian government, which instituted the system, have been a significant outcome of the Canadian Truth and Reconciliation Commission.[9] Lenny Duncan, in his 2019 book *Dear Church: A Love Letter from a Black Preacher to the Whitest Denomination in the US*, points to the South African Truth and Reconciliation Commission as a model for US churches and denominations and calls for reparations to nonwhite congregations and seminarians.[10] Some congregations are offering reparations. Memorial Episcopal Church in Baltimore began paying reparations in 2021 because it was built with funds from a plantation where hundreds of people of African descent were enslaved.[11] United Parish in Brookline (in Brookline, MA) launched the Negro Spiritual Royalties Project, through which the church pays voluntary royalties whenever spirituals written by people who were enslaved are sung in worship.[12] Reparations programs have also been initiated by several denominations and regional church bodies.

Another recent example of church-related reparations includes those paid by several religiously affiliated universities, including Georgetown University, Princeton Theological Seminary, and Virginia Theological Seminary, in recognition that these schools actively participated in and financially benefitted from the slave trade.[13] However, there has been criticism that the funds paid have not been sufficient to address all historical and ongoing oppression, nor have the schools adequately reckoned with their support of the theologies that justified slavery.[14]

Still, while making reparations might be a starting point, one-time payments are not sufficient to address the racial oppression in which white Christians and churches have participated and continue to participate. Political and economic change is clearly needed to address racial disparities. The church can and must advocate for this change, while at the same time reexamining its own theology and practices. Christian stewardship and church finance practices can serve as both a laboratory for and a foretaste of the broader societal change so urgently needed.

Decolonial Praxis and Church Finance

Decolonial perspectives also help us to look at the ways colonial histories and mentalities have shaped our financial practices. A decolonial approach to church finance begins by asking how churches came to be built where they are. As

I described in chapter 3, in the North American context,[15] we need to grapple with European migration, settlement, and colonization, and the roles played by various churches and theologies in that process. One part of this history is the doctrine of discovery, which is based on a series of papal bulls (decrees), particularly in the fifteenth century, that legitimized colonial land-claiming and violence against Indigenous peoples and spiritualities.[16] It stated that any lands not inhabited by Christians could be claimed by explorers for European monarchs and that Indigenous peoples who had not converted to Christianity could be killed or enslaved. In the United States, this doctrine was also enshrined into secular law. Many North American mainline Protestant denominations have repudiated this doctrine in official statements.[17] Yet issuing a statement is only a first step. The fact that these churches continue to exist on and profit from colonized lands and colonialism shows that there is much more to be done.

So, what can be done? A first step might involve building awareness of and relationships with the particular Indigenous nation(s) where a church is situated. Territorial acknowledgments, where the traditional Indigenous territory is named at the beginning of worship, meetings, in email signatures, and so forth can help to reframe understandings about place, although I caution churches against adding a territorial acknowledgment without taking any further action. Questions should be asked about how specific church financial holdings or assets have benefited from colonization. A wide-ranging analysis should look at church members' employment in colonially entwined industries (for example, government-related employment, resource extraction, and so forth), benefits church members and communities have received from colonization (such as cultural privilege, intergenerational wealth transfer, and so forth), and the specific wealth generated through the land and its location (for example, property value, rental income, and so forth). We should also strive to make amends for the negative impacts experienced by Indigenous peoples arising from their lack of access to church-owned properties and other outcomes of colonization (for example, cultural genocide, racism, ecosystem destruction, and so forth). Amends might be made through land return, reparations payments, and participating in Indigenous-led environmental stewardship practices. This work might be in some ways fraught and difficult, but we must remember that living as individuals and as a church in North America is not a neutral act. All property and wealth are entangled with colonization. And again, reparations emerge as a framework that can help to guide the process of striving toward right relationships and decolonization.

Colonial projects were not limited to European migration to North America, of course. The African slave trade was also deeply tied to colonialism, and ongoing international relations and global business and trade can be understood as colonialism in new forms (referred to as neocolonialism, through which many former colonial powers benefit greatly from present-day systems). Not all people who live in North America have benefited from colonialism to the same extent, if at all (and many have been significantly harmed). For example, many waves of immigrant groups have come to North America due to the impacts of colonialism on their homelands. These differing experiences of colonialism affect our responses to it. We need to take responsibility for our actions and the realities we have benefitted from (directly and indirectly). We also need to avoid speaking as though we're all the same, even with the intention of collective repentance for colonialism. But these complexities do not mean we should sidestep the issue. Most North American mainline Protestant denominations have European, and therefore colonial, roots, and therefore colonialism is part of our collective history and ethical responsibility.

We need to examine investments and other financial holdings to see how they may be connected to colonial and neocolonial projects around the world. We need to study global church mission histories and ongoing global church relationships. We need to grapple with the employment of church members in neocolonial projects around the world (for example, international finance, marketing, education, and development) and the ties then between those industries and our offering plates. Clearly, exploring colonial legacies is complicated work, and the process of disentangling colonization and church finance is not likely to ever be fully complete. Yet striving toward justice is itself valuable, and understanding how church finance is situated within the web of colonialism is a first step toward establishing right relations and social justice.

Environmental and Climate Justice

Church financial practices can also enhance our commitments to climate justice. We are participating in climate injustice through both action and inaction. Churches might be able to help heal our ecosystems instead of causing harm, however—for example, by divesting from fossil fuels, converting a lawn into a bioregionally specific garden, installing solar panels, minimizing electricity usage, offering programs online so people do not need to drive long distances to church, encouraging carpooling to church events, and giving staff more continuing education time so they can take a train to a conference rather than fly.

Often church finance is addressed on a relatively short-term horizon: we want to make this year's budget, and we want to track our trajectory year to year. When we do think about the long term, we want most to protect endowment fund investments, never touching the principle, so the fund can exist forever. Committing to environmental and climate justice encourages us to think about the long term in a critical and grounded way that takes seriously the stakes of the crisis. We need to understand what is likely to happen where we are located in the next five, ten, or fifty years, so we can think about how to best serve our communities. Can we become a resilience hub or emergency shelter? Can we model, teach, and resource the practices our members and our neighbors will need? How can we contribute to a positive ecological future, even if it might mean forgoing some of our financial security in the present? Eternal life is not a promise God made to our buildings, after all. Eternal life is a promise God made to us, and it is at least in part about the values that can and should persist after our lives, even if their specific forms look different.

Often one of the reactions I hear regarding climate action is that it is so expensive. "We'd love to do that, but we just barely get by as it is." And I understand that. Looking at the intersection of climate justice and social justice, we see that privileged individuals and churches are better able to afford the "flashy" purchases, such as eco-friendly electric cars, solar panels, and so forth. But we need to keep in mind that we're all in this together and there are many paths to becoming more environmentally just. Those of us with comparably greater privilege have the most responsibility to act—because we have the ability to do so and because we have contributed the most to the problem of climate change (a reality that the framework of climate debt reveals). This disparity might be addressed by wealth transfers between churches and organizations to ensure all have access to climate-related adaptation and mitigation measures.

We should also note that some climate action doesn't cost a lot: simpler living can make a significant difference. When people say climate action is too expensive, frequently the default is to just keep on doing what we've been doing. But that's often not the only possibility. Maybe rather than continuing to use fossil fuels to heat our poorly insulated building, we sell the building to an organization that can retrofit it and we become a renter in that space or, when possible, meet for worship outdoors. Of course, taking culture, climate, and other aspects of identity and context into account, we need to be aware that outdoor gatherings might not meet all needs or be accessible to all people. There are many creative possibilities, and many churches are also working to redevelop their spaces to make them more usable to their communities (by creating, for example, an event venue, offices, housing, and other rental spaces) in ways that might also generate the funds needed to become more climate friendly. Climate justice isn't just a nice thing to do when we can afford it. Like other forms of justice, it is required of us.

Principles for Justice-Based Christian Stewardship

We need to ask whether any stewardship or finance practice incarnates the transformative, transgressive, and liberative love of God, countering the forces of oppression, exclusion, inequality, and poverty in our world. Christian ethicist Maria Cimperman argues that social change and social justice must be embodied, imaginative, radical, and relational.[18] I believe that in matters of personal and congregational stewardship and finance, embodiment should encompass attention to privilege and oppression and how they impact churches, church members, and communities more broadly. This attention should lead to action, not merely statements of inclusion and acknowledgment of historical wrongdoing but also transformative changes that address injustice. Church finance should aim to imaginatively transcend the oppressive systems in our world, such as racism and neoliberal capitalism. We need not merely to address what is and has been but to establish new systems and ways of relating that will lead to greater justice. The principle of *radicality* requires that we pay attention to the root of the systems that operate in our world today and take seriously the radical potential of progressive and transformative Christian economic ethics, looking for any possible practical applications to church settings. Finally, the element of *relationality* refers to deep honesty in our conversations about individual and church finances that encourage us to share wealth and resources as acts of allyship and reparations. This practice is radically relational—crossing divisions, be they racial or spatial (geographical), or related to class, gender, theological perspective, denominational affiliation, sexual orientation, or any other source of division.

To approach church finance in a justice-rooted way requires Christian communities to support the needs of one another—to create communities where people need not fear scarcity because members have promised to manifest and incarnate God's abundance for and with one another. Of course, this is a significant project that we will not implement perfectly. Some might argue that it is foolish because it could lead to risk and disappointment, conflict and discord. Assessing the reality of situations, prioritizing needs, and ensuring the safety of all involved can be challenging.

Although this project might not be achieved in total perfection, it could take many smaller forms (particularly to begin with), including members providing goods and services to each other through bartering, gifts, interest-free loans, fundraising for one another's needs, offering housing, helping members find work, creating or supporting jobs or small businesses, caring for elderly members, and much more. Church members could work together to offer alternatives to student loans, payday loans, and credit card debt. Creating a significant safety net within congregations and interlinked pools among congregations in a neighborhood or within a denomination would serve as a foretaste of the world we are actively working to create for all people, perhaps by advocating at the same time for economic justice through legislative measures and mechanisms. If we want people to be generous with their resources and not to fear scarcity, we must create the conditions where scarcity is less prevalent and abundance is not only preached but incarnated.

We know there is precedent for profound sharing of resources within Christian communities. What if rather than focusing on institutional survival, we looked to the life, death, and resurrection of Jesus? We might be challenged to see that church closure or decline is not necessarily the worst outcome, particularly if resources are freed for other work—for new life. Theologian Kenneth Leech, in his writing on the crucified Christ, emphasizes the foolishness of the cross. He also notes that when he is tempted in the wilderness, Christ rejects worldly power and instead chooses "folly."[19] Leech argues that the church is called to follow in this example by serving as a sign of social contradiction rather than conformity.[20] Jesus's radical solidarity with the outcast is folly by the standards of the (privileged) world. Approaches to church finance should follow the way of Jesus, rooted in God's values rather than those of our present economy. Looking at our practices through the lens of the call to countercultural justice and solidarity, we have the incredible, life-giving opportunity to change our perspectives on what truly matters and to reimagine our practices in the service of our most central commitments: to bring forth love and justice, to serve God and neighbor.

5.

Justice-Rooted Church Finance
Foretasting the Kingdom

You may be wondering if any churches are doing the sort of work that I'm describing. Or you may be part of one of those churches already and want to consider what a next step might be. Personally, I feel encouraged when I hear about churches and communities doing this kind of creative work with money. I love hearing how communities are going against the grain and exploring together how principles of justice can be translated into community practices. And part of what I love is the variety and creativity of groups' efforts.

Abandoning the notion that everyone should use one best model, many of these communities are aware that what they are doing is both unique to their context and a work in progress. It's impossible to predict at the outset how things will go and what problems may arise. So, they just dive in and amend as they go. It's scary, of course. Sometimes things go wrong, feelings get hurt, critiques are raised. But if we wait until we've thought up the "perfect" approach before we get started with this work, we'll be waiting forever. And sometimes we might even use the desire to get it completely right as an excuse to delay. To prepare and research, consult and discern is wise. But our good desire to do things right can become a stumbling block when we are more afraid of a few potentially negative voices or unanticipated problems than we are motivated by the urgent needs around us. We need to trust that we can change course as needed and to err on the side of doing the best we can with what we know now. We need to prioritize the voices and feedback of those who are most marginalized and modify with their input as we go. We need to know that there is no one right way to do this work for every context. Instead of finding the one best way, we'll strive for diversity, creativity, and flexibility. Our practices will be more robust when we figure them out in community and include a deep awareness of the many aspects of our context. So, I share these examples not as "go and do likewise" models but rather to get your creative juices flowing about what might be possible where you are.

Debt Annihilation Program

Circle of Hope is a church with four campuses in the Philadelphia area. It has Anabaptist roots and a strong commitment to social justice. The church offers many small groups and hosts a variety of ministries, including a second-hand store, urban farm, counseling service, and programs related to racial justice, environmental justice, peacebuilding, and other issues.[1] One effort related to finance practices is their debt annihilation program, which the church initiated to pay off the credit card debts of their members.[2] The church formed three cohorts of six to ten indebted people, each of whom committed to practice complete financial transparency with others in their group, participate in financial coaching, stop using credit cards, and contribute to paying off the debts of everyone in the group.

The congregation provides seed funds to get the debt payment process started for each cohort and involves the larger congregation in supporting each cohort's efforts. This process of paying off debts begins with all cohort members contributing to pay off the debt held by the group member with the highest interest rate by giving a set amount directly to that person, enabling the group as a whole to pay less interest overall. At the same time, group members make minimum payments on all their own credit cards (for as long as they have any) to avoid penalties. The cohort lasts for as long as is needed to pay off every member's debts. This approach to debt payment results in a "snowballing" phenomenon, in which as soon as one card's debt was paid, that person's minimum payment funds were then devoted to paying off debt on another card in the group. As of 2019, over $100,000 of principle debt, plus interest, had been eliminated.

To learn more about the initiative, I spoke with Marguerite MacDonald, the ministry lead for the Circle of Hope Debt Annihilation Program. She participated personally in the second cohort of the program and has been an active leader ever since. She describes the program as "revealing Jesus incarnationally."[3] MacDonald shares that she had over $8000 in credit card debt herself. During her own participation in a debt annihilation group, she was the last in her cohort to have her debt paid because it had the lowest interest rate. She admitted that this required faith that her group would come through and continue to participate once their personal debts were paid off. MacDonald acknowledged the transformative impact the program had on her own life, fueling her desire to give back through leadership. She also explained that 20 percent of the overall church's budget goes toward a common fund to help people pay rent or bills or to provide small loans. The church has not yet established a strategy to deal with larger debts, such as student loans or medical debt, although they hope to do this in the future. For them, a core purpose of the program is to free up funds for people to contribute to the church and other charitable and justice-focused organizations, and to help people practice a radical version of stewardship by giving away before saving or spending.

MacDonald said that tithing is strongly encouraged in the congregation. About 20 percent of the church budget goes to its fund to support members' financial needs, and 20 percent is given to international ministries through denominationally related organizations.[4] When asked about any connections between the encouragement to tithe and the church's programs to help members experiencing financial needs, MacDonald said she believes people can be generous in their giving because they have the safety net of the church to support them and because they are encouraged and enabled to live more simply (for example, by using the church's thrift store), which frees up financial resources as well.

This is a powerful example of a church taking the real financial stresses of their congregation members into account and developing a transformative program to address them. Also, it does not merely support individuals one at a time but encourages people to come together and support one another. The wider congregation is also involved through seed monies for the cohorts, grants, and projects like the thrift store.

Although this approach doesn't fully address the complex systemic reasons some people are in debt and others are not (or to have less debt), it has real impact on people's lives. It inspires me to think about other examples where collective power could be used to minimize interest payments and even reduce debt creation in the first place. This church is thinking about all their financial practices through their commitment to justice, working to use their common funds to support the concrete needs of individuals, supporting alternative economies and simpler living practices, and extending their resources to give beyond their community and their congregation through denominational work.

Commoning, Reparations, and Jubilee

Agape Fellowship was founded in 2015 in Oakland, California, as a house church operating out of the home of one of the co-pastors. In 2018, they began to rent space in the East Bay Community Space, a multi-purpose venue that hosts a café and offers a variety of community programming, although the church closed in 2019. Their financial practices were unique and highly motivated by a commitment to social justice. Sarah Pritchard, who served as one of the pastors, described that their decision to neither own property nor pay their pastors/staff was in part "a way to concretely free up communities of ministry to think, 'Without the burden of paying a full-time pastor, what can we creatively do with our collective resources?'"[5] Although this choice might not make sense for all communities, I think it can expand our imaginations to at least consider the question.

At Agape, stewardship was understood primarily as "collectivizing resources" rather than funding the operation of the church, and decisions about funds were made collectively by members of the church at regular public meetings. Worshippers' offerings were divided into three categories: commoning, reparations, and jubilee. Commoning funds went toward the common expenses of the community, such as a Community Shared Agriculture food box that was used to prepare their weekly community meal, and their rent (once they moved into the East Bay Community Space). Reparations funds went to several Black, brown, and Indigenous organizations, including an Indigenous land trust and a home for recently arrived immigrants. The fund was understood as an act of wealth transfer from a primarily white congregation. Jubilee funds went to emergent community and congregational financial needs, which included paying the funeral expenses for a Black elder connected to the congregation and occasional bill payments for a marginalized family known to the community. Often these needs were brought forth by members of the Agape congregation who had relationships with people in need. Although in many ways this congregation's expenses were much less than most congregations, the primarily motivation for their model was not simply minimizing expenses. Pritchard described how the congregation decided to move from meeting in an apartment to the community space. Factors that went into the decision included making more visible expenses the pastors had previously simply absorbed (such as food and supply costs), which led more congregation members to contribute to them. The congregation also understood that meeting in a public space allowed them to do more outward-facing ministry and become better known in the community.[6]

Agape's model challenges our thinking about which expenses of typical North American mainline Protestant churches, particularly a building and paid staff, are indeed essential—and whether they are more beneficial than constraining. Agape's core budget categories are also provocative. Commoning is oriented toward the internal life of the community, reparations address privilege and structural inequality more broadly, and jubilee encompasses direct acts of significant impact for those in the local community and congregation, recognizing the structural injustice that often contributes to those needs. The jubilee category seems to be a bridge between both the commoning and reparations categories, using common resources to address needs that are often the result of systemic injustice. This approach to stewardship, while recognizing the greater privilege of many in the congregation, does not draw a firm line between givers/receivers or congregation members/others, and it suggests a great deal of flexibility and a participatory approach in determining where funds might be spent and how shared resources might be directed. I believe such categories and considerations would greatly benefit Christian stewardship more broadly.

Indigenous Leadership Toward Reconciliation

Denominations have amazing potential to redistribute resources across various divides. Even though the United

Church of Canada has done good work related to justice and finance—both within the denomination and with its global partners—the leadership of Indigenous peoples and churches in the denomination is especially exemplary. These leaders have called the denomination to use its structures, processes, and money to live into its commitments to reparations and reconciliation in a prophetic way—to embody word in deed.

The story of the relationship between Indigenous peoples and the church in Canada is deeply painful, marked by colonization, injustice, and inequality. A major aspect of this history is the Indian residential school system, which operated for more than 150 years and was attended by over 150,000 Indigenous children.[7] Attendance was mandatory, and children were removed from their families, taken far from home, forbidden from speaking their languages, separated from their siblings, and made to suffer many other forms of abuse, including malnutrition, physical abuse, and sexual, psychological, and emotional traumas. The schools also contributed to the deaths of many children, as recent discoveries of hundreds of unmarked graves at several schools have revealed. They were a tool of assimilation and cultural genocide.[8] The church and the state were very much aligned in this project, the government providing the (scant) funds for the schools and churches operating the schools.[9] The United Church of Canada, formed of Presbyterian, Methodist, and Congregationalist Churches in 1925, inherited twelve residential schools and thirty-nine day schools from the Methodist and Presbyterian churches. Other schools were run by the Catholic Church (via a variety of Catholic religious orders and organizations) and the Anglican church.[10] The last school closed in 1997.[11]

Thanks to the leadership of Indigenous peoples, the United Church has offered formal apologies to Indigenous communities and participated in Canada's Truth and Reconciliation Commission (2008–2015). Indigenous United Church of Canada leader Alf Dumont writes that the American Indian Movement of the 1960s led First Nations people in the United Church to find their voices to critique European theology and practices, particularly by organizing eleven consultations between 1979 and 1988 that ultimately called on the denomination to offer an apology.[12] A first apology was offered in 1986 and a more specific apology about residential schools was given in 1998. These apologies moved the denomination—led by Indigenous members—to call on the government to also apologize and make amends.

The United Church's 1986 apology was not without controversy. Some within the church were afraid of possible lawsuits and bankruptcy arising from admitting fault.[13] More important, Indigenous peoples within the church, through the Indigenous denominational structure, the All Native Circle Conference, acknowledged but did not accept the apology.[14] They responded in part: "The Native People of The All Native Circle Conference hope and pray that the Apology is not symbolic but that these are the words of action and sincerity."[15] The Indigenous church's governing bodies have continued to say that they are still waiting for sufficient actions that embody the church's stated apology. The funding and organizational structure of the United Church has been an important aspect of this journey toward reconciliation and justice. The All Native Circle Conference (as a nongeographic Indigenous organization, different from the geographically based regional church Conferences) was established in 1988 out of the desire for greater Indigenous autonomy and leadership within the church.[16] In 2008, the Aboriginal Ministries Council (now the National Indigenous Council) was established in a related effort.

After the United Church reorganized in 2018, a coalition of Indigenous church members demanded the right of Indigenous church communities to choose how they relate in the new church structure and called for the right to participate in both a regional church body and an Indigenous church organization. The Indigenous church has repeatedly called for respect and accommodation for Indigenous autonomy and use of consensus-based decision-making processes, and there are several ways that has been accomplished. They initiated an Indigenous Office of Vocation with a specific Indigenous Candidacy Board to support Indigenous ministry training and preparation and to represent Indigenous members on the denomination's Board of Vocation. Indigenous self-governance is increasingly a focus and a commitment for the denomination due to this leadership.

A 2019 Indigenous Gathering issued various demands to the denomination. Their statement begins with an acknowledgment of the detrimental impact of the Doctrine of Discovery, which "rests on the illegitimate claims of Christian superiority in the Papal Bulls of 1453, 1454 and 1493." These papal bulls contributed to and justified the colonization of the lands now known as Canada, and as a doctrine this has now been repudiated by the United Church.[17] The statement also notes that, as the church becomes smaller and properties are sold, the "sale of United

Church properties involves Indigenous claims to the land."[18] Therefore, the very presence of the United Church should be viewed through the lens of the Doctrine of Discovery, and when properties are sold, this history should be considered when determining to whom the land should be sold or transferred and where proceeds of sales should be directed.

Finance is an area of struggle with respect to reconciliation, justice, and right relations, and it is clear that funds are needed from the wider church to support ministry in communities that have been severely and negatively impacted by colonization, racism, and the ongoing intergenerational impacts of trauma such as residential schools. The missionaries who built the early churches for Indigenous communities in Canada promised to maintain the buildings and provide ministers.[19] However, declining funds have resulted in reduced support for both ministry personnel and building maintenance. Also, of the sixty-two Indigenous ministries in the United Church in 2015, only thirty had paid ministry personnel, some of whom were students or retired ministers.[20] But currently the United Church's funding is in a precarious position as church membership declines. Despite this, responding to Indigenous leaders, the United Church has committed to maintain the current level of financial support for Indigenous ministry and right relations work, protecting Indigenous ministry from funding cuts that would affect other parts of the denomination.[21] They also made the commitment that "the United Nations Declaration on the Rights of Indigenous Peoples will inform financial decisions that affect the Indigenous Church."[22]

Although the denomination has heard Indigenous voices and responded with financial commitments, much more needs to be done. For example, while commitments have been made to provide financial support to Indigenous churches and church bodies, the current level of funding is inadequate, given the overall economic disparity and the weight of historical and ongoing racism and colonialism. Also, while these commitments have been made to Indigenous churches, other racialized and marginalized communities need financial support. The overall structure of the denomination still requires that for the most part congregations are self-funding. This leads to significant budget inequalities as congregations remain largely segregated by factors such as class and race. In addition, some forms of ministry are not well suited to self-funding, such as community outreach ministries, prison chaplaincies, and global partnerships designed to serve marginalized populations. Still, the work that has been done by Indigenous leaders has moved the denomination toward financial justice and reparations, inviting the denomination to move toward practices that are more integrated with its justice commitments.

Reimagining Fundraising from Within

Community-Centric Fundraising is a new approach to nonprofit finance rooted in commitments to justice. The movement arose out of a 2015 article by social-justice activist Vu Le critiquing traditional fundraising models and approaches. In the article, "Winter Is Coming, and the Donor-Centric Fundraising Model Must Evolve," he describes how the donor-centered model (related to the notion that the donor is always right, examined in chapter 2), predominant in the fundraising world, is problematic. This model presents donors as the sole heroes of an organization's work, caters to them like royalty rather than challenging them, and sets up competition rather collaboration among organizations. The article led people of color involved with fundraising in Seattle to meet to discuss alternatives and eventually to create the Community-Centric Fundraising movement.

The movement has ten key principles, which include that fundraising should be rooted in structural and systemic analysis and address the hierarchy among nonprofits that privilege large, well-funded groups and marginalize smaller ones that tend to be led by people of color. Organizations need to focus on big-picture goals rather than individual missions, strive to support other organizations and collaborate, and ensure that they are accountable to the communities they serve. Staff should be paid and treated fairly, volunteers should be appreciated just as much as donors, and clients of services should be valued and viewed as more than just recipients of services (for example, by including them on boards and in other decision-making processes). Donors should be challenged when appropriate and should not be placed above the communities being served. The narrative that donors are "saviors" needs to be challenged, and stereotypes about the work being done and who is being served must be avoided. The focus must be on the root causes of injustice and inequality rather than merely their secondary impacts (a critique which arises in work related to the nonprofit industrial complex). The movement hosts events and shares information and resources for fundraisers and organizations striving to work in these and other more justice-rooted ways.

Churches are unique among nonprofits (and their nonprofit status is itself something to examine, as we considered in chapter 3), but this movement and its principles are helpful and relevant for churches that are seeking more just financial practices. Many of the issues, trends, and challenges we experience in churches are not unique to our organizations. True, in churches, we don't generally have a firm divide between staff, board, donors, and "clients." However, the tendency to be donor-centered has certainly impacted churches. Participants in the Community-Centric Fundraising movement believe this shift toward donor-centrism has both pros and cons. It is good to think about donors as more than "ATMs" (a source of funding and nothing more) and to ensure that those who are giving are treated respectfully. But both churches and other nonprofits tend to cater to donors (especially major givers) in ways that may undermine an organization's values or give donors an outsized voice in decisions. The need to work collaboratively rather than to focus solely on our own church and its own needs and desires applies to churches as well as to other nonprofits. A collaborative church, for example, might recommend that a visitor or member consider a different church that could be a better fit for them, rather than try to keep every visitor or member—especially big givers. Such a church might pass along information about a grant that would really help another church—or even possibly help them with the application materials if they need it. While churches might be wise to draw on practices from other fields, such as fundraising, we need to pay attention to those within them most committed to justice. While we might be tempted to adopt models from "successful" big nonprofits or businesses, we must remember that our call is not to be successful but faithful.

Other Local Church Initiatives

You may have read through these sections and be wondering how your community can practice justice in its finances. Many possibilities exist. For example, if your church is establishing a capital campaign, you could commit to giving a set percentage to a more marginalized faith community or nonprofit organization that might not have the ability to undertake such a campaign themselves. You could practice wage transparency, giving all church members and employees access to everyone else's salary information. This could also be part of an initiative in which all church members, meeting in small groups, share information with one another about their own finances and financial situations. These open conversations are among the practices of groups associated with the Iona Community, an ecumenical Christian community based in Scotland. One of their practices, to which members commit, is "accounting with one another for the use of our gifts, money and time, our use of the earth's resources."

Making one's financial situation public, at least to a few people, can be an important first step to determining who is paid a just wage and who is not, and making change where it is needed. It can also be a first step to learning about the financial stresses and quandaries faced by people in your congregation and imagining how you could offer support and foster mutual solidarity. You could require that a certain

number of church finance committee members fall below a
certain income level. You could give away some percentage of your weekly offering to other organizations in the
community or designate Sundays when the whole plate
offering is given away. You could develop a relationship
with an organization in the community and ask what your
church might do to support them (for example, by offering
free meeting space, volunteering for events, and so forth).
You can address financial concerns and economic justice
issues in your preaching, teaching, and prayers and begin
to create a culture (and specific forums) where people ask
for what they need and offer what they can to one another.
These are just a few ideas, and I am sure you can think of
others that might resonate well with your context and the
work you are already doing.

Your Own Community

How might these examples relate to your own church or
community? I know reading examples and case studies
can be helpful and inspiring, but it can also be challenging.
Sometimes I think it might be easier to start a new church
(like Agape Fellowship) or focus on one activity, such as
fundraising, rather than juggling the many roles and tasks
that church leaders undertake. If you're feeling stuck in
patterns and traditions or feeling pulled in multiple directions, I hear you. My best advice is to build a team of folks
both within and outside your church to work with you.
Don't try to do it alone. You might encounter people who
have been involved with church finance work, who have

sensed for some time that the conventional approach just doesn't sit right, and who are energized by something new. People who have never been involved with financial ministries might be excited by them when they are approached in a new way. Whether experienced or new to fundraising, the people working with you can be a sounding board, a support network, and a source of new perspectives. They might also be doing this work in their other communities (and possibly professional lives) and be eager for support and conversations about justice that can inform their efforts. One of the tensions we face is that while change might take time and be only incremental, the needs in our world are great and urgent. So, we need to do the best we can and work for the long haul, knowing we won't always get it right but that trying counts.

Every step toward more just practices matters. Each step toward the service of God is a step away from the service of money. These steps might seem small, but we can have faith that small things, like the mustard seed in Jesus's parable, can transform into something big. Just because we see that more could be done doesn't mean we shouldn't do what we can now. Jesus often healed individual people while, at the same time, proclaiming a vision for a transformed world. Even if a new approach to our finances makes a difference in the life of only one person or one creature on Earth, that is still valuable. We shouldn't get complacent with this kind of impact if we are indeed capable of more, but neither should we think that small impacts don't matter. The in-breaking of God's kingdom is already happening, and it is not yet complete. While we imagine grand prophetic visions of what could be, we must do the patient and persistent work to make those visions real. Even small steps toward that vision are still better than no steps at all. Sometimes the journey toward justice creates its own momentum as others catch a spark of the vision and join in. And we can always trust that God does much with little; we are never alone in this work.

6.

Our True Calling

Embracing God's New Life

This is a difficult moment for many churches, especially those in mainline Protestant traditions. I don't need to go on about declining numbers and declining resources. Chances are, you know this all too well, and many books have already been written on that topic. But you might think that because congregations are struggling with decline, this isn't the right time to experiment with church finance. It might sound interesting, but there doesn't seem to be enough energy, resources, time, or people to examine our financial practices. Better to hunker down and hold on to what we have, not to take risks. However, I think "business as usual" might hasten our demise. Further, I think many churches are smaller and less powerful than they once were, our communities are becoming more religiously diverse, and the fact that most people who don't want to go to church no longer feel social pressure to do so might be a good thing.

Even apart from underlying practical concerns related to decline and change in mainline churches, we can't keep doing what's been done before. Our faith compels us. And rather than acting as though decline is inevitable and unavoidable, we need to take stock of what we do have and can still do. This might be a time when we should also think creatively and collaboratively, rather than thinking of our individual churches in isolation. And rather than avoiding bold risks and acting as though our churches have already closed, we need to explore the good we can now do (without getting too focused on whether the specifics are permanently sustainable). We should not succumb to the temptation to romanticize a time when some churches were full. Christendom, an era of deep interconnection between the church and powerful forces in the world, often involved churches supporting colonialism, racism, and other oppressive systems and forces. This support might even have led many people away from the church. Now that the church is a little further from the centers of power, though, we might be better able to see our true calling: to stand with the marginalized rather than the powerful. People might not rush back to the church if we change, but that cannot be our primary motivating factor. This work of bringing our practices into alignment with our values is important for its own sake—and our faithfulness to the gospel. Our churches may still close or struggle regardless of what we do with our finances—so why not go out boldly and as faithfully as we can?

As money is so central to the contemporary social order, alternative financial practices can be highly subversive, helping to fundamentally reshape our congregations and our wider communities. That reshaping needs to take place on multiple levels and must include us as individuals and families. Money woes and financial stresses make up a huge part of our lives and take up a lot of our time and mental energy, even for those of us who are relatively well off. If we are all thinking about money a lot of the time, though, why don't we talk about it more in church? These conversations about church finance and our present economic structures can be liberating for individuals and enable them to better understand the dynamics and contexts we are impacted by. They can make it possible for people to draw together to support one another in their financial challenges.

One reason we sometimes avoid conversations about money is that we are afraid to offend—or to admit the ways that we have been and are offending by participating in economic injustice. One feature of some mainline congregations is a desire to offer a "big tent" and to avoid taking a stand on difficult topics. As we discussed in chapter 1, denominations and ecumenical organizations may release powerful statements on difficult topics, but many individual congregations avoid talking about potentially divisive issues. But in trying to be all things to all people, we may end up being nothing to anyone—or at least nothing of much importance. Jesus wasn't impartial in situations of injustice, and we need to find the courage to follow his lead.

So just how do we do this work of integrating justice and church finance? You might have picked up this book hoping that I would tell you exactly what to do. A lot of stewardship books promise that—ten easy ways, five simple tricks, and so forth. But this work of integrating justice fully into church finance isn't simple. Justice must be deeply integrated into the whole life of a church. We cannot make little adaptations and then keep doing everything else as we have in the past. Integrating justice into church finance also needs to be contextual. It needs to arise out of each church's identity, location, history, resources, and both internal and community needs. Not every church is the same. We don't all have the same responsibilities, possibilities, or callings. At the same time, we are also not as different from one another as we sometimes think. We might not all have the same specific call, but all our callings are part of one overarching call to manifest God's call of love and justice in our communities. I propose that most churches can apply a few overarching principles rooted in just financial practices, albeit in their own unique ways. Inspired by the principles of Agape Church's financial practices (described in chapter 5), I will explore reparations, jubilee (as well as sabbath), and commoning as three aspects of justice-rooted church finance that could help shape practices in many contexts.

Reparations

We've already discussed reparations in previous chapters, especially chapter 4, so I will revisit the topic briefly. In order to engage in reparations, we first need to look long and hard at the ways that we, directly and indirectly, have upheld and contributed to injustice as individuals, congregations, and as a part of the wider church. We can't do this work in isolation; we need to hear the voices of those both within and outside our churches who have less power now and had less power in the past. We need to hear their stories and perspectives on what we have done, are doing, and can do going forward. The work of reparations requires entering into deep relationships, attending fully to those who have been harmed, listening to what they say they need from us, opening ourselves to ongoing critical feedback, and joining in solidarity to address whatever struggles might be going on today.

In our church life, part of that work needs to involve budgets, buildings, staff, investments, and other assets. For example, if we are going to seek reparations with a LGBTQ+-affirming church community that our congregation split from over that stance, we need to do more than simply acknowledge in a statement that we are sorry. We should think about the material resources that community was denied and seek to make amends through redistribution of assets. We need to show our support actively and ask what we can do to both demonstrate our repentance for the past and enter into common cause now. That might include following their lead and helping to create a LGBTQ+ youth shelter, in collaboration with them rewriting congregational history and the story of the split, advocating with them for just and inclusive denominational policies, offering funds to compensate for the years they had to rent space for worship, providing free space for meetings and programming going forward, and exploring whether we might become one church community again. We need to know that trust might not come immediately and some of our offers may be turned down. But thinking creatively about how we might make amends for the past, demonstrate our commitment to learning and growth, and work collaboratively for justice now can show that our hearts have truly changed.

Much is said about the importance of taking a first step. While it is true that a first step is necessary, we also need to make sure that we commit to going beyond merely "a start" and not become complacent with what we have already done. Reparation needs to be an ongoing commitment and one that is continually revisited. We also need to examine reparations in light of not only other people but also the entire expanse of creation, including the intersection of social justice and ecology, and humans' role in climate change and ecological devastation. As we engage in reparations with other species and the Earth itself, we need to also consider which human communities are most impacted by climate change. We must be sure our actions for reparations do not further marginalize but rather support and empower these communities and their local ecosystems. While we need to proceed with caution, reparations with both human communities and the Earth is a faithful response to our recognition that we have been (directly and indirectly) a source of harm.

As we discussed in chapter 4, reparations related to racism and colonialism are important for many churches in North America, and there are many communities engaging in this work right now that we can look toward for inspiration. These include communities examining the ways they benefitted from slavery and colonialism, participating in truth and reconciliation initiatives, and making royalty payments to Black communities and organizations for the use of African American spirituals in worship. When engaging in reparations, we need to consider where our financial assets have come from, who built our buildings, what industries we have invested in, and which struggles for justice we have been absent from. In order to move justly into the future, we need to contend with our past. Although some harm cannot be repaired, at least not completely, making reparations is a framework that can help us to make amends for what has been and enter into the relationships we need to ensure we can minimize harm in the future. When thinking about our church finances, we need to consider reparations first. We so often treat our justice commitments as an afterthought, or, at best, as an important and worthy option for funds we have left over after our "core" ministries are paid. But work to repair harm and offer recompense for injustice should be at the beginning of our financial considerations, not left to the end.

Sabbath and Jubilee

In the Hebrew scriptures, sabbath refers to periodic times of rest (the seventh day and the seventh year, primarily) and jubilee to the practice of forgiving debts, returning sold land, and freeing prisoners and slaves (in the forty-ninth year, after seven cycles of seven years). These two concepts are distinct but clearly interwoven: both involve release from oppressive patterns and structures, a "reset button" so inequality and exhaustion are not reinforced. Both are about saying no and no more, this is enough and that is sufficient, it's time to pause and wipe the slate clean. This approach can apply to church finance in many ways. We might stop certain projects, ministries, or other aspects of our life together because they no longer serve, have become a burden, or may be oppressive in some way. We might give our building to a community organization that can make better use of the space and more easily maintain it or give land back to Indigenous organizations or communities in recognition that, in a jubilee year, things are returned to those whose ancestors held them. We might discontinue an annual mission trip that plays into a "white savior" complex or has a negative ecological impact. We might sell investments in products or services that cause harm. We might forgive loans we have made to a person or the debts of a rental organization. On a more individual level, we might help church members consider what the concepts of sabbath and jubilee could mean for their own lives and work, and support them in taking up practices that reflect those callings.

We might support sabbath-minded release and relief from unjust burdens for people who have become caught in debt cycles. RIP Medical Debt is a campaign that uses donated funds to buy bundled portfolios of medical debts and pays off the debt, freeing the debtor from the obligation. These debts are generally held by people at or near the poverty line. The organization was founded by Craig Antico and Jerry Ashton, who used to work in debt collection and saw how these debts caused tremendous hardship. They knew these debts can be bought at a steep discount when done on a large scale, because the creditors recognize those in debt are unlikely to ever pay in full and so are willing to accept a small percentage of the money owed. Once the debt has been paid, the organization simply sends a letter to inform those whose debt has been paid. This allows that person to rebuild their credit score and to redirect their resources and time toward other priorities. There are no strings attached, and people do not need to apply for the relief. Many churches have participated in this campaign out of the belief that no person should have to go into debt to obtain medical care, and those churches have contributed to a fresh start for thousands of people. This can be understood as an example of jubilee—offering a fresh start and cutting off cycles of indebtedness.

Church life itself can also be infused with a spirit of sabbath and jubilee. Some churches take sabbaticals from committee meetings periodically or at certain times of the year. In some cases, this might simply recognize that many people will be taking holiday time over the summer, but congregations might explore the practice with an eye toward justice. What might it mean to have a whole committee take a sabbatical from their meetings and instead rest and pray for their ministry? What bold ideas or insights might emerge? What practices might we view differently, with refreshed minds? Many denominations offer pastors a sabbatical after a certain number of years of service. This important spiritual practice could be extended to other paid staff and volunteer leaders. What if we periodically offered our custodians, nursery workers, treasurers, and others a sabbath, in addition to vacation time and other established practices for rest and renewal? Sometimes time away from the everyday grind is just what we need to approach our lives, relationships, and work in ways that are more compassionate and just.

As a creative interpretation of jubilee, what if we restarted our churches (and denominations?) from scratch every forty-nine years? What might we do differently if we were truly starting anew? If many churches did this all at once, what new partnerships and collaborations might emerge between them? Of course, you might be thinking this could never happen, but I invite you to consider it as a thought experiment. If you were starting a church from nothing, how would you do it? What might that new church be like? When I think about re-creating church practices to be most just, the hardest part for me is thinking about how to get from what exists now to what could be. How much easier to start something new than to incrementally make change after change. If we knew that after forty-nine years we were going to give away everything we had, how might we approach resources differently? Churches, like people, generally follow certain stages of development and, some argue, have limited lifespans. Discerning when to take stock and knowing whether now is the moment to make a major change—to close, merge, reinvent, or recommit to what is—can be difficult. An externally imposed timeline might be a catalyst for asking those big, foundational questions (and remove the common temptation to postpone change). And the spirit of sabbath and jubilee, focused on giving away what has been accumulated, freedom from oppression, and a period of rest before starting again, might help to reshape us toward more just practices.

Commoning

In chapter 1, we discussed the witness offered in Acts where members of the young Christian community pooled their possessions and distributed them to any as they had need. What does that mean for our churches today? We can enact this passage by bringing together some or all of what we have (including money, resources, skills, abilities, time, and so forth) and sharing these assets with those most in need. Most churches do some form of commoning on some levels (think about potluck meals—or even just the ordinary practice of taking up an offering)—but we can go much deeper. We can place more of what we have in the common pool to create a more robust and vibrant communal safety net and a fund to work collectively. At the simplest level, this might include a larger and more abundant benevolence fund to support financial needs of members or others known to the community. We might also create free libraries for food, tools, toys, cooking implements, and so forth; skill-sharing and repair workshops; matching forums where people can post both offers and needs; even intentional communities for small groups of people to live together. Intentional communities have found many ways to hold resources in common and this can even be practiced by people who don't live together, such as some small group ministries. For example, certain household items might be owned by a group, meals might be prepared by group members on a rotating schedule, and tasks such as childcare might be coordinated and done collaboratively. When we pool our resources, skills, needs, and dreams, we free up resources to live more deeply into our individual and collective vocations.

Tension can sometimes arise between directly meeting the urgent needs of those most marginalized and creating a collaborative and interdependent culture where all are both givers and receivers. Creating such a culture challenges the dominant social context. Some people might not want to get too involved, thinking the effort is risky and preferring not to make themselves vulnerable enough to do so. Although people often respond with generosity when a specific need is presented, people who are struggling might not want to ask for help and think their needs are their own private responsibility, so those who could help don't know the need exists. Giving a tax-deductible donation to an organization is easy (when you know you can spare it), but lending (or collectively owning) an item that might get broken or lost can be tough. Feelings can get hurt, trust can be broken. Giving, knowing we might be asked again (and again and again, and maybe for more next time!)—not simply thanked for our generosity—can make us feel awkward, especially if we know we have a lot more than others in our community and perhaps more than we should. But these aren't insurmountable challenges. We can share both a vision and a mechanism to create a culture that supports commoning. We can describe the many reasons holding things in common is better for the planet, for deepening relationships, for building a life that is more creative and interesting, and for promoting greater peace of mind, knowing that the community will support us as we have supported others.

We can also common beyond our local community. Through denominations, regional church bodies, ecumenical and interfaith organizations, community networks, and activist movements, we can and should common on a wider scale. Inequality tends to be greater across larger areas—our local community will be more economically homogeneous than our state, country, or world—and therefore the power of redistributing resources across wider boundaries is that much more important. As I mentioned in chapter 2, I've been active in both churches and community organizations in which people who are relatively privileged have offered one another (for free!) time at vacation homes, expensive baby gear, nice furniture, theater tickets, rooms for rent at a low cost—and all that is great, a beautiful example of an impulse to share.

However, I can't help but think how this practice allows relatively privileged folks to increase their privilege by saving money, while more marginalized folks are much less likely to have access to these sorts of things through their networks. In some marginalized communities, people sometimes feel like they are all just trading their last twenty bucks on one another's crowdfunding campaigns, or lending each other the same blazer to wear to job interviews. How can we make sure our practices of commoning cross these divides of inequality and oppression? One way is through social change and political advocacy work. As churches, of course, we are not ultimately responsible for replacing government services or allowing governments—that is, us (at least those of us with legal status)—to shirk our responsibilities to ensure a strong social safety net. We need to advocate for strong policies in areas such as health care, education, unemployment assistance, disability benefits, child tax benefits, and so forth.

We need to think and act globally. Racism, colonization, ecological devastation, and other issues divide countries and regions of the world. We in the Global North have benefitted tremendously from these systems. As Christians and as churches, we have been complicit. We have contributed to the devaluation of many spiritualities and cultures, and to the economic and social divides that persist. We have benefitted from cheap energy and consequently owe a climate debt to those in the Global South, whose lives are affected by the many crises that climate change is accelerating and exacerbating. If we truly believe we are all one human family, one body of Christ, how can we not be concerned about anyone's suffering—no matter how geographically far away? If we are one church universal when we pray, how can we justify keeping our funds and resources separate? If we don't believe that "what's mine is mine," how can we justify acting as if "what's ours is ours?"

When working with others, many of us feel some hesitation about engaging with churches in other parts of the world out of our shame and regret for our missionary past and our support of colonialism and racism. Many of us have allowed this discomfort, and the desire to honor the autonomy of churches in the Global South, to serve as an excuse for us to not share as radically as we could. Instead, many of us have focused our outreach primarily in our local communities, which has felt less fraught, less likely to entrench power differentials, and less complicated. But that doesn't mean we don't have global ethical responsibilities, especially as we continue to participate in systems, from our shopping habits to our work lives to our government diplomacy and beyond, that further marginalize those in the Global South. We must think about commons and commoning in the broadest possible way, not satisfied to share solely with those who are near and dear. Only when we are commoning across every division will the truly radical potential of Christian financial practice be realized.

New Life for Churches

I hope after reading this book you are persuaded that we need to align our ethical commitments and our church practices. The feminist slogan "the personal is political" also captures the importance of analyzing specific, personal, and local financial practices in light of larger structures and realities. Other common sayings, such as "practice what you preach" and "practices preach," communicate the many ways actions often speak louder than words. North American mainline Protestants have a long history of engaging intellectually on issues related to justice and advocating for a more just society. But if our own practices do not demonstrate our commitments to justice, we are undermining the gospel message of equality, transformation, and hope. While church decline is real and can be very painful, it can also be a force for positive change if it is taken as an opportunity for radical reformulation and refocusing on our values rather than on conventional markers of success, such as attendance numbers or budget size.

A central theological and biblical theme of Christian life is that in dying we find new and eternal life. In Matthew 16:25–26, Jesus proclaims: "For those who want to save their life will lose it, and those who lose their life for my sake will find it. For what will it profit them if they gain the whole world but forfeit their life?" This teaching is at the center of my own faith life, and I believe it is particularly instructive for church financial practices. By trying to "save" our churches through capitalist, colonial, and white supremacist approaches to finance, we are already dead because we have ceased to be the church, Christ's followers. But if we cease to fear the death of the church, if we no longer allow that fear to dictate our choices, if we turn instead to living by our radical commitments to economic justice, we may well discover that we find new life. That "life" may not be full pews and offering plates.

We cannot predict exactly what that life will look like, but we can trust in the promise of it. God says, "I am about to do a new thing; now it springs forth; do you not perceive it?" (Isaiah 43:19). Perhaps the new life we will find will be in greater relevance to our wider communities, more creative and just practices that witness to our faith, or more transformative impact on the lives of church members and other people. This shift may mean the closure of some churches and perhaps even the end of some denominations. But if longevity, attendance, and budget size are not our metrics of success, we could be freed for new definitions of success. This creative renewal is possible, and it is already taking place. The time is right for us to recognize and embrace the new life God is offering us.

Notes

Territorial Acknowledgment

1 This territorial acknowledgment is based on that of the UC Berkeley Centers for Educational Justice and Community Engagement. For more, see University of California at Berkeley, "Ohlone Land," accessed September 7, 2020, https://cejce.berkeley.edu/ohloneland.

Introduction

1 For more, see World Council of Churches, "Racism, Discrimination, and Xenophobia," accessed May 19, 2021, https://www.oikoumene.org/what-we-do/racism-discrimination-and-xenophobia.

2 For example, see David Masci, "How Income Varies Among US Religious Groups," Pew Research Center, October 11, 2016, accessed June 28, 2022, https://www.pewresearch.org/fact-tank/2016/10/11/how-income-varies-among-u-s-religious-groups/.

3 Michael Lipka, "Why America's 'Nones' Left Religion Behind," Pew Research Center, August 24, 2016, accessed June 28, 2022, http://www.pewresearch.org/fact-tank/2016/08/24/why-americas-nones-left-religion-behind/.

4 Pew Research Center, "Faith in Flux," April 27, 2009, accessed June 28, 2022, http://www.pewforum.org/2009/04/27/faith-in-flux/.

5 See, for example, Joe Pettit, "Blessing Oppression: The Role of White Churches in Housing Apartheid," *Journal of the Society of Christian Ethics* 40, no. 2 (Fall/Winter 2020): 291–309.

Chapter 1

1 Ched Myers, "From Capital to Community: Discipleship in Jesus' Parable about a Manager of Injustice (Luke 16:1–13)," in *Radical Christian Voices and Practice: Essays in Honour of Christopher Rowland*, eds. David B. Gowler and Zoë Bennett (Oxford: Oxford University Press, 2012), 56–57.

2 Ched Myers, *". . . and distributed it to whoever had need": The Biblical Vision of Sabbath Economics* (Washington, DC: Tell the Word, 2001), 41–45.

3 Cynthia Moe-Lobeda, *Resisting Structural Evil: Love as Ecological-Economic Vocation* (Minneapolis: Fortress Press, 2013), 58.

4 Richard A. Horsley, *Covenant Economics: A Biblical Vision of Justice for All* (Louisville, KY: Westminster John Knox Press, 2009), 102.

5 Horsley, *Covenant Economics*, 143.

6 Horsley, 178.

7 World Communion of Reformed Churches, "Accra Confession," 2004, accessed December 1, 2018, http://wcrc.ch/accra.

8 World Communion of Reformed Churches, "Accra Confession."

9 World Communion of Reformed Churches, "Accra Confession."

10 World Communion of Reformed Churches, "The Accra Confession," 2004, accessed December 1, 2018, http://wcrc.ch/accra/the-accra-confession, para. 27.

11 World Council of Churches, "Alternative Globalization Addressing People and Earth (AGAPE)," February 14, 2006, accessed December 1, 2018, https://www.oikoumene.org/en/resources/documents/assembly/2006-porto-alegre/3-preparatory-and-background-documents/alternative-globalization-addressing-people-and-earth-agape.

12 World Council of Churches, "Alternative Globalization Addressing People and Earth (AGAPE)."

13 World Council of Churches, "Alternative Globalization Addressing People and Earth – AGAPE A Call to Love and Action," September 2005, accessed December 1, 2018, https://www.oikoumene.org/en/folder/documents-pdf/pb-06-agape.pdf, 1.

14 World Council of Churches, "Alternative Globalization Addressing People and Earth – AGAPE A Call to Love and Action," 2.

15 World Council of Churches, "Alternative Globalization Addressing People and Earth – AGAPE A Call to Love and Action," 7.

16 World Council of Churches, "Alternative Globalization Addressing People and Earth (AGAPE): A Background Document," April 2005, accessed December 1, 2018, https://www.oikoumene.org/en/folder/documents-pdf/agape-new.pdf, 28, 30, 35.

17 Patricia Hill Collins and Sirma Bilge, *Intersectionality* (Cambridge, UK: Polity, 2016), 85.

18 Ibram X. Kendi, *How to Be an Antiracist* (New York: One World, 2019), 13.

19 Traci West, *Wounds of the Spirit: Black Women, Violence, and Resistance Ethics* (New York: New York University Press, 1999).

20 Traci West, *Disruptive Christian Ethics: When Racism and Women's Lives Matter* (Louisville: Westminster John Knox, 2006), 121.

21 West, *Disruptive Christian Ethics*, 114.

22 West, 118.

23 James Cone, *Black Theology and Black Power*, 2nd ed. (New York: Seabury Press, 1989), 3.

24 Néstor Medina, "A Decolonial Primer," *Toronto Journal of Theology* 32, no. 2 (2017): 279.

25 Many nation-states and place names, including that of North America, are themselves colonial constructs and impositions.

26 Medina, "A Decolonial Primer," 282.

27 Glen Coulthard, "Place Against Empire: Understanding Indigenous Anti-Colonialism," *Affinities: A Journal of Radical Theory, Culture, and Action* 4, no. 2 (2010): 79.

28 Coulthard, "Place Against Empire," 80.

29 Lynn White, "The Historical Roots of Our Ecological Crisis," *Science* 155 (1967): 1203–207.

Chapter 2

1 David Harvey, *A Brief History of Neoliberalism* (New York: Oxford University Press, 2007), 5–7.

2 Harvey, *A Brief History,* 64–69.

3 Mark Allan Powell, *Giving to God: The Bible's Good News about Living a Generous Life* (Grand Rapids, MI: William B. Eerdmans Publishing Company, 2006), 3.

4 Kevin DeYoung, "Social Justice and the Poor (1)," The Gospel Coalition, August 19, 2009, accessed June 1, 2022, https://www.thegospelcoalition.org/blogs/kevin-deyoung/social-justice-and-poor-1/.

Chapter 3

1 Joe Pettit, "Blessing Oppression: The Role of White Churches in Housing Apartheid," *Journal of the Society of Christian Ethics* 40, no. 2 (Fall/Winter 2020): 299.

2 See Ched Meyers, ed., *Watershed Discipleship: Reinhabiting Bioregional Faith and Practice* (Eugene, OR: Cascade Books, 2016).

3 To learn more, visit Sogorea Te' Land Trust, accessed June 22, 2021, https://sogoreate-landtrust.org/.

4 To learn more and to read about more examples of churches returning land, see Emily McFarlan Miller, "Churches Return Land to Indigenous Groups as Part of #LandBack Movement," *Religion News Service,* November 26, 2020, accessed June 22, 2021, https://religionnews.com/2020/11/26

/churches-return-land-to-indigenous-groups-amid
-repentance-for-role-in-taking-it-landback-movement/.

5 Ana Clarissa Rojas Durazo, "We Were Never Meant to Survive," in *The Revolution Will Not Be Funded: Beyond the Non-Profit Industrial Complex*, ed. INCITE! Women of Color Against Violence (Boston: South End Press, 2009), 116–17.

6 Rojas Durazo, "We Were Never Meant to Survive," 117.

7 Zildo Rocha, *Helder, o dom: uma vida que marcou os rumos da Igreja no Brasil* (Petrópolis: Editora Vozes. 1999), 53.

Chapter 4

1 Barbara Rossing, "Models of *Koinonia* in the New Testament and Early Church," in *The Church as Communion: Lutheran Contributions to Ecclesiology*, ed. Heinrich Holze (Geneva: Lutheran World Federation, 1997), 65.

2 Rossing, "Models of *Koinonia*," 66.

3 Rossing, 66.

4 Rossing, 68.

5 Rossing, 70.

6 Rossing, 75.

7 Lawrence H. Williams, "Christianity and Reparations: Revisiting James Forman's 'Black Manifesto,' 1969," *Currents in Theology and Mission* 32, no. 1 (2005).

8 Williams, "Christianity and Reparations."

9 Kim Stanton, "Canada's Truth and Reconciliation Commission: Settling the Past?" *The International Indigenous Policy Journal* 2, no. 3 (2011): 3, https://doi.org/10.18584/iipj.2011.2.3.2.

10 Lenny Duncan, *Dear Church: A Love Letter from a Black Preacher to the Whitest Denomination in the US* (Minneapolis: Fortress Press, 2019), 45.

11 Michela Moscufo, "Churches Played an Active Role in Slavery and Segregation: Some Want to Make Amends," NBC News, April 3, 2022, accessed May 4, 2022, https://www

.nbcnews.com/news/nbcblk/churches-played-active-role
-slavery-segregation-want-make-amends-rcna21291.

12 Craig LeMoult, "This Church Is Paying 'Royalties' When
It Sings Spirituals Composed by Enslaved Africans,"
GBH News, November 16, 2021, accessed May 4, 2022,
https://www.wgbh.org/news/arts/2021/11/16/this-church-is
-paying-royalties-when-it-sings-spirituals-composed-by
-enslaved-africans.

13 Ed Shanahan, "$27 Million for Reparations Over Slave
Ties Pledged by Seminary," *New York Times*, October 21,
2019, accessed October 24, 2019, https://www.nytimes.
com/2019/10/21/nyregion/princeton-seminary-slavery
-reparations.html.

14 Shanahan, "$27 Million for Reparations."

15 Even the term "North America" is a colonial relic (as is the
case with both the terms "United States" and "Canada" and
the names of many countries, cities, towns, states, and so
forth). Alternative terminology for places such as "Turtle
Island" or the Indigenous terminology that relates specifically to the land where a church is situated may be more
appropriate. Examining the history of place names and
church names specifically is an important aspect of decolonial praxis.

16 See, for example, Doctrine of Discovery, "What Is the
Doctrine of Discovery?," accessed July 2, 2020, https://
doctrineofdiscovery.org/what-is-the-doctrine-of
-discovery/.

17 Doctrine of Discovery, "Faith Communities," updated
January 6, 2020, accessed July 2, 2020, https://
doctrineofdiscovery.org/faith-communities/.

18 Maria Cimperman, *Social Analysis for the 21st Century*
(Maryknoll, NY: Orbis Books, 2015), 29.

19 Kenneth Leech, *We Preach Christ Crucified: The Procla-
mation of the Gospel in a Dark Age* (Cambridge, UK and
Boston, MA: Cowley Publications, 1994), 15–16.

20 Leech, *We Preach Christ Crucified*, 10.

Chapter 5

1 Circle of Hope, "Compassion Teams," accessed July 2, 2020, https://www.circleofhope.net/compassion-teams/.

2 Joshua Grace, "My Church Came Together to Pay Off Each Member's Debt," *Sojourners*, July 2019, accessed July 6, 2022, https://sojo.net/magazine/july-2019/my-church-came-together-pay-each-members-debt.

3 MacDonald interview, November 12, 2019.

4 MacDonald interview, November 12, 2019.

5 Sarah Pritchard, interviewed by author by phone, December 3, 2019.

6 Sarah Pritchard, interview, December 3, 2019.

7 National Centre for Truth and Reconciliation, "Residential School History," accessed July 17, 2022, https://nctr.ca/education/teaching-resources/residential-school-history/.

8 Truth and Reconciliation Commission of Canada, 2015, "Honouring the Truth, Reconciling for the Future," accessed October 10, 2019, http://www.trc.ca/assets/pdf/Honouring_the_Truth_Reconciling_for_the_Future_July_23_2015.pdf, 1.

9 Alf Dumont and Roger Hutchinson, "Church Mission Goals and First Nations Peoples," in *The United Church of Canada: A History*, ed. Don Schweitzer (Waterloo, ON: Wilfrid Laurier University Press, 2012), 222–23.

10 Truth and Reconciliation Commission of Canada, 2015, "Honouring the Truth, Reconciling for the Future," 3.

11 Truth and Reconciliation Commission of Canada, 2015, 70.

12 Dumont and Hutchinson, "Church Mission Goals and First Nations Peoples," 223.

13 Martha Troian, "25 Years Later: The United Church of Canada's Apology to Aboriginal Peoples," *Indian Country Today*, August 16, 2011, accessed July 6, 2022, https://indiancountrytoday.com/archive/25-years-later-the-united-church-of-canadas-apology-to-aboriginal-peoples.

14 The United Church of Canada, "The Apologies: We Have Already Travelled Far Together," accessed November 1, 2019,

https://www.united-church.ca/social-action/justice-initiatives/apologies.

15 The United Church of Canada, "The Apologies."

16 The United Church of Canada, "Caretakers of Our Indigenous Circle: Calls to the Church," July 2018, accessed August 1, 2022, https://sandysaulteaux.ca/wp-content/uploads/2018/02/caretakers-indigenous-circle-calls-church.pdf, 7.

17 The United Church of Canada, "Caretakers of Our Indigenous Circle," 10.

18 The United Church of Canada, "Caretakers of Our Indigenous Circle," 10.

19 Kristine Greenaway, "'We Can Now Refloat the Canoe' Says Canadian Indigenous Residential School Survivor," The World Council of Churches, October 15, 2015, accessed July 6, 2022, https://www.oikoumene.org/en/press-centre/news/201cwe-can-now-refloat-the-canoe201d-says-canadian-indigenous-residential-school-survivor-1.

20 Greenaway, "We Can Now Refloat the Canoe."

21 The United Church of Canada, "New Funding Model Summary," accessed 1 August, 2022, https://united-church.ca/sites/default/files/new-funding-model-summary.pdf, 1.

22 The United Church of Canada, "New Funding Model Summary," 6.

Recommended Resources

Books

Day, Keri. *Religious Resistance to Neoliberalism: Womanist and Black Feminist Perspectives.* New York: Palgrave Macmillan, 2016.

In this academic but accessible book, Day introduces the concept of neoliberalism and its impacts, and presents critiques rooted in Christian faith and Black feminist/womanist analysis.

Dowd, Elle. *Baptized in Tear Gas: From White Moderate to Abolitionist.* Minneapolis: Broadleaf Books, 2021.

This memoir calls on white Christians to transform our relationship with justice concerns into a central component of our lives, overcoming the socialization and privilege we have been raised with.

Duncan, Lenny. *Dear Church: A Love Letter from a Black Preacher to the Whitest Denomination in the US.* Minneapolis: Fortress Press, 2019.

As a pastor, Duncan writes to the church and shares a compelling vision of how the church can find vitality by actively pursuing racial justice in both society and church practice.

Graeber, David. *Debt: The First 5000 Years.* Brooklyn and London: Melville House, 2014.

Graeber provides a broad overview of society's relationship to the economy, and specifically the concept of debt, over many time periods and in many cultures. He analyzes the theoretical interconnections between religion and finance and provides much context for understanding our contemporary economic situation.

Heath, Emily. *Courageous Faith: How to Rise and Resist in a Time of Fear.* Cleveland: Pilgrim Press, 2017.

As a progressive pastor, Heath encourages Christians and churches to face our fears and take bold stands against oppression and for justice.

INCITE! Women of Color Against Violence. *The Revolution Will Not Be Funded: Beyond the Non-Profit Industrial Complex.* Cambridge, MA: South End Press, 2007.

This compilation shows how the model of nonprofit organizations emerged, how nonprofits relate to work for justice today, and why we need to think critically about them.

Janzen, David. *The Intentional Christian Community Handbook: For Idealists, Hypocrites, and Wannabe Disciples of Jesus.* Brewster, MA: Paraclete Press, 2013.

This practical guide provides a starting place for those interested in forming intentional communities in the Christian tradition. It offers advice both for new communities as they are forming and for communities that already exist.

Kendi, Ibram X. *How to Be an Antiracist.* New York: One World, 2019.

This popular book combines personal stories from Kendi's life with an analysis of how racism operates and what can be done about it. It underscores the need to look at actions, not simply feelings, when considering whether something or someone is racist.

Kim, Grace Ji-Sun, and Susan Shaw. *Intersectional Theology: An Introductory Guide.* Minneapolis: Fortress Press, 2018.

This accessible theological book introduces the concept of intersectionality from a Christian theological perspective. It shows how the concept can inform how we approach our faith and our lives in communities.

Moe-Lobeda, Cynthia. *Resisting Structural Evil: Love as Ecological-Economic Vocation.* Minneapolis: Fortress Press, 2013.

Moe-Lobeda argues that ethics needs to focus on not only the actions of individuals but also the systems that we are embedded within, and broadens our scope to consider all species and the Earth itself.

Sit, Tyler. *Staying Awake: The Gospel for Changemakers.* St. Louis: Chalice Press, 2021.

Sit presents a variety of practices Christians and churches need to attend to in order to follow Jesus's instruction to "stay awake" and respond prophetically to the injustices of the world.

Other Resources

AGAPE Statement and ACCRA Confession

These statements of the World Council of Churches and the World Communion of Reformed Churches, respectively, address issues of global social justice from a Christian perspective. Both were drafted by a broad coalition of churches, particularly prioritizing voices from the Global South, and were officially endorsed by many mainline denominations.

World Council of Churches. "Alternative Globalization Addressing People and Earth (AGAPE)." https://www.oikoumene.org/en/resources/documents/assembly/2006-porto-alegre/3-preparatory-and-background-documents/alternative-globalization-addressing-people-and-earth-agape (accessed July 6, 2022).

World Communion of Reformed Churches. "Accra Confession." http://wcrc.ch/accra (accessed July 6, 2022).

Ched Meyers/Bartimeus Institute

Ched Meyers is a biblical scholar and theologian who integrates theological concepts such as sabbath and discipleship with justice practices. I particularly recommend these texts (the first is a short booklet).

> *The Biblical Vision of Sabbath Economics.* Washington, DC: Tell the Word, Church of the Saviour, 2001.
> *Watershed Discipleship: Reinhabiting Bioregional Faith and Practice.* Eugene, OR: Cascade Books, 2016.

The Bartimeus Kinsler Institute, an annual event that "provides an opportunity for interactive and in-depth study of scripture and social justice in the Ojai Valley, CA," is co-hosted by Ched Meyers and his partner Elaine Enns and friends. https://www.bcm-net.org/study/bartimaeus-institute (accessed July 6, 2022).

Communities

There are many intentional communities around the world where people live together as they strive to share resources and life rooted in Christian faith. These include the Catholic Worker movement and L'Arche (focused on adults with intellectual disabilities). A new organization, Community of Peace, in Louisa, VA, welcomes people for shorter time periods and is inspired by the Taizé Community in France. One example of another form of community is the Iona Community in Scotland, a place of retreat/pilgrimage that also supports nonresidential small group communities around the world. One practice of these small groups is transparency with one another about their personal use of time, skills, money, and natural resources.

> The Catholic Worker Movement: https://www. catholicworker.org/ (accessed July 6, 2022).
> L'Arche International: https://larche.org/ (accessed July 6, 2022).
> Community of Peace: https://www.communityofpeace. org/ (accessed July 6, 2022).
> The Iona Community: https://iona.org.uk/ (accessed July 6, 2022).

Community-Centric Fundraising

This movement and approach to fundraising is rooted in justice. Practitioners strive to "prioritize the entire community over individual organizations, foster a sense of belonging and interdependence, present our work not as individual transactions but holistically, and encourage mutual support between nonprofits." https://communitycentricfundraising. org/ (accessed July 6, 2022).

Dismantling the Doctrine of Discovery

This Anabaptist-based compilation contains many resources related to Indigenous justice and particularly repudiating the Doctrine of Discovery, a legal doctrine supporting European colonialism that was endorsed by the church. The website contains links to a documentary film, study guides, a speakers' bureau, and more. https://dofdmenno. org/ (accessed July 6, 2022).

Festivals

In addition to the Bartimeus Institute, several festivals bring together justice-focused people of faith. The Wild Goose Festival is a four-day spirit, justice, music, and arts event held each summer in North Carolina. Cahoots, a four-day faith, justice, and "DIY" (do-it-yourself) event, is held each summer in Ontario, Canada. https://wildgoosefestival.org/ https://www.cahootsfest.ca/ (accessed July 6, 2022).

Geez Magazine

Geez is "a quarterly, non-profit, ad-free, print magazine about social justice, art, and activism for people at the fringes of faith." Issues deal with topics such as imagining jubilee, joy as resistance, dismantling white theology, and communing with trees. https://geezmagazine.org/ (accessed July 6, 2022).

Lilly Family School of Philanthropy: Lake Institute on Faith and Giving

This organization does research related to philanthropy in religious organizations and offers a variety of educational programs on the topic, including a Certificate in Religious Fundraising. https://philanthropy.iupui.edu/institutes/lake -institute/index.html (accessed July 6, 2022).

Mutual Aid

Mutual aid is a practice by which neighbors and community members support one another's needs with free gifts of household items, practical assistance, disaster relief support, and more. Its popularity spread in many communities during the COVID-19 pandemic. This website can help you learn more and locate a project near you. https:// www.mutualaidhub.org/ (accessed July 6, 2022).

Native Land Digital

This interactive online map shows the Indigenous territories, languages, and treaties in much of the world. New content is regularly added. The site also offers information about Indigenous territorial acknowledgments. https:// native-land.ca (accessed July 6, 2022).

RIP Medical Debt

This organization uses funds from donors to buy bundled portfolios of medical debt in order to provide relief to those who have incurred the debts. As of 2022, they have assisted 3.6 million people with collective debts totaling over $6.7 billion. https://ripmedicaldebt.org/ (accessed July 6, 2022).

Wendland-Cook Program in Religion and Justice

This is an interdisciplinary program based at Vanderbilt University Divinity School focused on issues related to religion, economics, and ecology. It offers programs for students, activists, religious leaders, and others to dialogue and work together for a more just world. https://www .religionandjustice.org/